Indoor Bonsai
for Beginners

Werner M. Busch

Indoor Bonsai for Beginners

Selection · Care · Training

WARD LOCK

Indoor Bonsai for Beginners

A WARD LOCK BOOK
First published in the UK 1997 by Ward Lock. Wellington House, 125 Strand, London WC2R 0BB
A Cassell imprint
ISBN 0 7063 7583 1

Reprinted 1998, 1999, 2000 (twice)

© 1995 by Falken-Verlag GmbH, 65527 Niedernhausen/Ts.

Translation: Andrew Wilson in association with First Edition Translations Ltd, Cambridge
Photos: BASF, Limburgerhof Agricultural Research Institute: 45 r., 46 l.; **Bonsai Centrum Heidelberg,** Mannheimer Straße 401, 69123 Heidelberg: 33; **Friedrich Jantzen,** Arolsen: 42, 43 (2x), 45 l., 46 r., 47 (3x); all others: **Daniel Meyer-Horn,** Düsseldorf (page 1: Ulmus parvifolia; page 2: Punica granatum; page 3: Punica granatum 'Nana')
Illustrations: FALKEN Archiv/Lünser: 19 (3x), 23 (2x); all others: Daniela Schneider, Frankfurt am Main

Printed and bound by Pozzo Gros Monti S.p.A. - Turin - Italy

Distributed in the United States
by Sterling Publishers Co., Inc.
387 Park Avenue South,
New York, NY 10016-8810

Contents

Why indoor bonsai?

The term bonsai means a plant, usually a tree or shrub grown in a container, that is made to look like a mature tree through the use of various training techniques. The plant usually does not exceed one metre in height.

However, few people seem to realize this, since the image most of us have of a bonsai tree is influenced by the specimens we most commonly see. These are not the fully developed, meticulously trained masterpieces produced by experts, but the mass-produced articles sold in do-it-yourself stores, shopping malls, and garden centres. Unfortunately, these often very cheap products have as little to do with the true art of bonsai as a single word with a poem or a block of stone with a marble statue. They have usually not been trained but at most pruned just once, and look more like a stunted plant than a mature tree.

In order to be able to judge what you have in front of you, a good deal of experience and knowledge of the subject is required.

The first bonsai trees that found their way to Europe came from Japan. In their new climate, however, Japanese trees had to be kept outdoors all year round. Then more and more people heard about the art of cultivating miniature trees, and began to look into the matter more thoroughly. It is reasonable to assume that those who had no garden or even a balcony concentrated their efforts on plants that would flourish indoors. It was not long before such plants began to be imported from China.

Trees have held a particular fascination for human beings since time immemorial, and they have been the subject of numerous stories, legends, and songs. For anyone without a garden, bonsai offers a wonderful opportunity to become involved with some of nature's most impressive creations. This involvement may simply be a form of indoor gardening, but it can also have its artistic side. Part of the fascination of bonsai lies in the exotic origin of the plants. But it also offers indoor gardeners an opportunity to extend their knowledge of botany and to apply it to the plants they cultivate. This calls for creativity. And connoisseurs can build up a collection that will adorn their homes in a most impressive way. Indoor bonsai is indeed a hobby with a great deal to offer.

Feroniella lucida, *about forty years old, Rüger collection*

Buying indoor bonsai trees

The origin of the plants

Anybody wishing to buy an indoor bonsai tree should pay particular attention to the origin, quality of training and age of the plant, as well as its suitability for use as an indoor bonsai.

Most of the commercially available indoor bonsai trees come from China. They are usually imported in very loamy soil adorned with small rocks on which dainty clay figures are stuck. Once the plants have been imported, they are kept in greenhouses for a few weeks. Because of the rigours of their long journey and the different climate to which they now have to adjust, they usually shed all their foliage in the greenhouses and begin to sprout new leaves. Only then are they put on sale.

The loamy soil they are planted in is unsuitable if the miniature tree is to be kept indoors, because it becomes so heavily compressed with repeated watering that the roots suffocate and die. So immediately after purchase, the loamy soil has to be replaced by a different soil mix. This should preferably be done in stages, with part of the original soil being replaced first, followed a few weeks later by the rest. Plants will tolerate the change of soil particularly well if the new soil contains a lot of fired clay particles. These retain their granular structure well and prevent the soil from becoming too compressed.

However, many bare-rooted plants are imported from all over the world and are then immediately planted in a suitable soil. Once the plants are firmly rooted, they are put on sale.

Other plants are propagated locally, grown to a suitable size, and then supplied to retailers. Such plants are often fairly young when bought and are easily trained.

The quality of training

The indoor bonsai trees that are available commercially have usually not been properly trained, and have often only been shaped very roughly. Even plants with thick stems have often not been trained, but simply kept small and treelike by fairly severe pruning.

Such crude treatment can often be improved upon if the tree is not already too old. Unfortunately, really well-trained bonsai trees are relatively expensive.

Nevertheless, if you decide to invest in such a tree, the Japanese styles will give you a good idea of the quality of training. These are described on pages 15 to 18.

Age

The older a bonsai is, the more firmly established the shape becomes. So if you want to train a tree yourself, the plant you buy should not be too old.

The age of a plant can usually only be estimated. However, as it has a considerable effect on price, the plant's age will obviously affect your decision as to which tree to buy. The thickness of the trunk and the sophistication of the training can be used as guidelines to age. A powerful trunk that has no trace of rough pruning along its entire length, from root to tip, can be assumed to be very old, while a trunk of similar thickness with large, open cuts is usually only a few years old. The more clearly defined the shape appears to be, and the more refined the branching, the older the plant is.

Suitability as an indoor bonsai

Most of the plants suitable for use as indoor bonsai trees come from the tropics or subtropics, where they are kept outdoors, not inside. These plants are naturally adapted to the climate of their native countries. However, many prove to be flexible in their requirements. Bonsai lovers with little experience should initially stick to these varieties, or to those that are accustomed to a climate that can be easily recreated in the home. These more flexible species are mainly the different varieties of fig trees (*Ficus*), but also include the myrtle (*Myrtus communis*) and the Chinese podocarpus (*Podocarpus macrophyllus*).

The demands of some subtropical plants can easily be met by not heating the room in which the plants are kept in winter. Such plants include the pistacias (*Pistacia lentiscus*, or mastic tree), the olive tree (*Olea europaea*) and the myrtle (*Myrtus communis*).

Before buying a bonsai, you should in any event seek advice in a specialist shop. Bonsai experts can usually state with a high degree of accuracy which plants will flourish in which locations.

Ficus panda, *about three years old*

Eugenia, about ten years old. Its requirements are the same as those of Myrtus communis

Ficus benjamina, *about thirty years old, Rüger collection*

Training an indoor bonsai tree

Anyone who becomes a serious devotee of bonsai will hardly be likely to buy a fully developed specimen that requires no more than a little maintenance.

Much of the fascination of this hobby is derived from the experience of watching a plant grow and of repeatedly intervening in the process in order to train it to grow in a particular style. So in this section we shall describe in detail how to grow a bonsai from the very beginning.

The structure of a bonsai

Every bonsai tree consists, ultimately, of as harmonious a blend as possible of the following elements: bonsai container, soil surface, rootage, trunk, branches, foliage and flowers.

A wide range of bonsai containers is available commercially

The bonsai container
The minimum requirements for a bonsai container include holes in the bottom and small feet, so that excess water can drain away. The container and the plant should form a harmonious whole. Success in this respect depends partly on personal taste and partly on the plant's stage of development. Young plants, for example, are best suited to a container that actually seems too big for them, because this will allow them room to develop more quickly.

It is often the case that only mature and expensive specimens are found in their optimal pots, the glaze of which often matches or complements the colour of the tree or bark structure.

The following rules of thumb should be applied when choosing the size of container: either the length of the container should be about two-thirds the height of the tree, or the height of the tree should be about two-thirds the length of the container.

The proportions will seem all the more harmonious if the crown of the tree extends to the edges of the container but does not extend beyond them. The container should be approximately as high as the bottom of the trunk is thick.

Soil surface
A beautiful bonsai should have a soil surface to match.

If the plant is kept outside during the warmer months, a carpet of moss usually develops on the surface of the soil. The dry atmosphere indoors, however, will cause the moss to shrivel up.

This is why other plants are used as groundcover to keep the soil surface looking green. Mother of thousands (*Soleirolia soleirolii*) has proved suitable for indoor and outdoor use. Small ferns and many other plants well suited to adorning the soil surface are available commercially. The surface can also be decorated with small stones.

Rootage

A good bonsai should have good surface roots that actively tie the trunk into the ground. This is a characteristic of older trees growing in their natural environment. The roots are one of the most important elements in the design of a bonsai, and visible roots are essential for

all bonsais. An ideal arrangement can be achieved if those roots growing straight downwards from the trunk and not contributing anything to the desired radial formation are cut back a little further every time the roots are trimmed. If this is done properly, the side roots (which are the ones that form the aesthetically pleasing radial arrangement) will have to supply the whole tree with the nutrients it requires, and will gain in strength as a result.

Trunk

The trunk should be thickest at the base and should taper well, narrowing gradually all the way from the base to the apex. This is usually achieved by pruning the trunk severely several times while the tree is still young. The branch closest to the cut then becomes an extension of the trunk and thus the apex of the tree. The greater the intervals between each pruning, the larger the

Such a splendid carpet of moss will flourish only when humidity is high

The different varieties of Ficus *develop particularly strong surface roots*

Ficus microcarpa *with a very expressive trunk (Rüger collection)*

11

cuts will be. Large cuts indicate a method of cultivation that is aimed primarily at achieving a thick trunk. This is a legitimate and widely used method of creating a plant suitable for cultivation as a bonsai. The cuts should be treated with wound sealant so that they heal up as quickly as possible.

A good, fully developed bonsai has no open cuts, so that any traces of earlier pruning will be virtually invisible.

Branches

The ideal bonsai has fine, sturdy branches with correspondingly thinner secondary branches. The more secondary branches there are, the more

With regularly pruning, even young plants can be encouraged to develop a delicate tracery of secondary branches and twigs (Ulmus parvifolia, Thönnessen collection)

fully developed the tree is. A well-shaped bonsai has thicker branches at the bottom and thinner ones at the top. The branches strike out from the trunk and ramify (divide into smaller branches) towards their tips, with the secondary branches becoming lighter and lighter the further they are from the heaviest part of the branch. This is achieved by pruning each branch severely at regular intervals, in the same way as the trunk. The secondary branch closest to the cut then becomes the tip of the branch.

The more a branch grows before it is pruned, the thicker it will become. This is why branches closer to the apex of a bonsai are pruned earlier than those lower down, so that the lower branches are the thickest, as they would be on a naturally growing tree.

Foliage

The leaves should, of course, look vigorous and healthy. Small-leaved varieties of trees are usually preferred to any others, although leaf size can vary considerably depending on the tree's stage of development. With a young tree, leaf size is unimportant, since priority should be given initially to developing the tree's shape. However, developing the shape usually requires vigorous growth, one of the consequences of which is that the leaves will grow to a normal size.

The smaller the leaves, the easier it is to achieve a harmonious relationship between the size of the leaves and the size of the tree. With large-leaved varieties, the size of the leaves can be reduced by encouraging ramification. The smaller the secondary branches, the smaller the leaves become.

One important method of reducing leaf size by encouraging ramification is leaf cutting. This involves stripping off

Alternate leaves

all the leaves but retaining the stalk or petiole. Afterwards, a new branch will grow at every point where there used to be a leaf; if all the new branches sprout evenly, they will bear leaves that are usually somewhat smaller than the ones that were cut off. However, this technique should be used only on healthy trees that already have a sturdy trunk, since it is very debilitating and can even retard the development of the trunk.

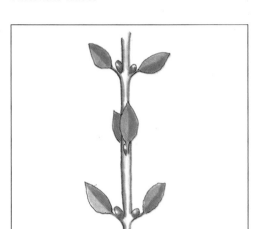

Opposite leaves

1. The leaves are cut off at the stalk

2. The new leaves are somewhat smaller than the ones previously removed

Spiral leaves

13

Flowers

Flowers enhance the appearance of a bonsai in a most charming way, but they have very little to do with the quality of the shaping process, since even a completely untrained plant will flower once it has reached a certain age. So flowers can only complement a design, never really improve it. For this reason, the primary objective in cultivating a good bonsai should always be to develop the shape, leaving any flowers to bloom later of their own accord. When trees are in bloom, their rate of growth usually slows down to an absolute minimum. A vigorously growing tree, on the other hand, produces very few flowers. So if trees are fed large quantities of nitrogen to encourage growth, flowering is likely to be inhibited.

A pomegranate in flower (Punica granatum)

The Japanese styles

The long-established Japanese bonsai tradition has led to the development of recognized styles for shaping or training trees. These styles are based on naturally occurring growth patterns.

Anyone wishing to train a bonsai of their own will find it very useful to take these Japanese styles as a starting point. However, it should be remembered that they only serve as a guide. Every plant has its own particular characteristics that mark it out unmistakably as an individual, and it is this individuality that is the hallmark of an impressive bonsai.

Broom style
In this style, the trunk does not serve as the main axis of the tree from the ground right through to the apex; rather, it divides up from a certain point into branches of more or less equal thickness that spread out in all directions to form a compact circular, oval, or umbrella-shaped crown. The trunk is usually upright and has a uniform appearance all the way round, i.e. there is no obvious back or front.

Upright style
This style comprises a group of shapes in which the trunk serves as the main axis all the way up from the base to the apex of the tree. In this style, there is a clear distinction between the back and front of the tree. Viewed from the front, the branches strike out from the trunk alternately from the left and right-hand sides. The branches are usually horizontal or slightly drooping. The bottom branch should also, as far as possible, be the thickest, and the branches should get thinner the higher

Broom style

Upright style

15

up the tree they are. Depending on the shape of the trunk, a distinction is made between the formal upright style, in which the trunk is absolutely straight, and the informal upright style, in which the trunk may have kinks or twists that impart a sense of movement.

Slanting style

In this style, the trunk has a pronounced slope to one side. In other respects, this bonsai is similar in shape to the upright style: the branches are horizontal or slightly drooping and emerge from the trunk alternately from the left and right-hand sides.

Twin trunk style

In this style, two trees grow out of one root. One of the trunks should be large and sturdy, the other smaller and more delicate. The branches emerge horizontally from the two trunks to form a common crown.

Twin trunk style

Slanting style

Multiple trunk style

Multiple trunk style

This style follows the principles of the twin trunk style, but more than two trees (usually an uneven number) emerge from the single root. Here too, the individual trunks vary in thickness and height. As far as possible, the smaller trunks should have the smaller branches and the larger trunks should have the larger branches. The branches of all the trunks form a common crown.

Raft style

Group or forest style

Raft style

In this style of bonsai growing, the branches emerging from a trunk half buried in the soil are trained to resemble individual trees, but with partially separate crowns.

Group or forest style

In this style, several individual trees, usually an uneven number, are planted together in one container. This style can vary considerably, depending on how the trees are arranged and how the trunks are shaped.

Cascade style

This style, in which the direction of growth is downwards, is inspired by trees growing out of cliff faces and rock crevices. In the semi-cascade style, the tip of the trunk is located between the edge and the bottom of the container,

Cascade style

17

while in the full cascade style, the tip extends beyond the base of the container. Cascade trees are usually grown in fairly high containers in order to create an impression of stability.

Literati style

The literati style is characterized by a particularly striking, slim, tall trunk that is also the main feature of the design. The shape of the trunk is often reminiscent of those depicted in pen and ink drawings. The branches are usually confined to the upper third of the trunk and are small in number.

Propagating a bonsai from seed

Bonsai shops, as well as specialist seed shops and garden centres, often have so-called bonsai seeds for sale. This term is confusing. All such seeds are nothing other than ordinary tree seeds, from

Literati style

which a perfectly normal tree will grow unless it is trained in the way that all plants have to be trained to become a bonsai.

Cultivating bonsai from seeds is a very laborious but engrossing business. It is not a method to be recommended to beginners, since it is generally very difficult to grow trees from seed. They often die after a few months, and the whole process has to start all over again.

The effort is worthwhile only in the case of plants that cannot be obtained as cuttings or young plants, or with varieties that are easier to grow from seedlings than from cuttings (see the table on pages 26–7).

In many cases, a seed capsule brought back as a souvenir after a trip can be the starting point for an attempt to cultivate a tree from seed.

Only a few types of seed should be allowed to dry out after they have matured. These seeds are mostly those of conifer trees. Once gathered, they should be stored in a dry, well-ventilated place until the spring and then sown. Berries should be placed in water for a few days until the beginnings of a fermentation process can be observed. The flesh can then be separated more easily from the actual seed. Once the seeds have been detached from the flesh, they should be sown immediately and the seed tray placed in a warm spot. To obtain good results, it is usually necessary to treat the soil surface with a fungicide.

Some seeds need time to mature before they are ready to germinate. Most oak seeds fall into this category. The best thing is to sow them immediately after gathering and to place the seed trays in a frost-free but cool spot for the winter.

The best medium in which to sow the seeds is ordinary potting compost, which usually consists of sand and peat. The compost should be kept moist at all times, but never soaking wet. As soon as the seeds begin to sprout, the soil surface should be kept as dry as possible, with the only water coming from below. Place the seed tray in a container filled with water that will keep the compost above the drainage holes in the tray suitably moist.

About four weeks after germination, you can begin to add fertilizer. Use an inorganic fertilizer, but reduce the quantities indicated on the packet by half.

Once the plants have grown so much that they are beginning to crowd each other out, they must be transplanted. Take them out of the tray and plant them out separately. As you do so, remove any tap roots that may be present to encourage the growth of side roots. Do not prune the plant itself in the first year. Basic training and shaping should not begin until the second year.

Propagating a bonsai from seed

2. Cover the seed with a thin layer of soil, press in firmly, and water

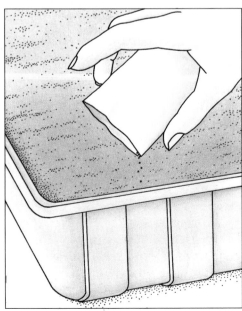

1. Sowing: distribute the seeds evenly around the soil-filled container

3. As soon as the first leaves emerge, the seedlings should be planted out

19

Shaping an upright tree without wire
With the first cut, the future trunk is given its first change of direction. The height of the trunk, the position of the first branch, and the total height of the tree can also be established at the same time (Figure 1).

In a healthy one-year-old seedling, such pruning will (at least) cause the two buds closest to the cut to erupt, sometimes even more. The upper shoot will become the leader (i.e. the continuation of the trunk), while the lower one will develop into the first branch (Figure 2). Any additional shoots should be removed entirely. The branch should be cut back to a third of its length when it has grown as long as the trunk is high. All subsequent branches should be pruned in the same way.

When the trunk is at least twice as high as the distance from the soil surface to the first branch, it should be cut back (Figure 2). The remaining section should be a little shorter than the length that remained after the first pruning. The

3   4

1   2

5

20

second cut should be made in such a way that the second bud from the top points in the opposite direction to that in which the first branch is growing. After budding, this will become the second branch (Figure 3), while the shoot nearest to the cut will become the leader and be pruned when it has reached the appropriate length. The third branch will develop at the point where the third cut is made (Figure 4). If pruning continues in this way, a distinctive branch pattern emerges, in which the secondary branches strike out from the trunk alternately from the left and right-hand sides (Figure 5). At the same time, each cut changes the direction of the main trunk line, thereby creating an impression of movement that will ultimately determine the expressiveness and character of the bonsai.

Shaping an upright tree with wire

If you train your seedling with wire, you will eventually produce a tree with a noticeably tapering trunk. Begin by bending the seedling to one side at exactly the point at which the first cut is made in the method described in the preceding section (Figures 1 and 2).

Once it has been bent in this way, the tip will continue to develop as a secondary branch.

Once the bud closest to the bend has erupted, the new shoot will become the leader (Figure 3). The first secondary branch should be cut back several times and kept short. Once the main trunk has reached a certain height, it too should be

3

1   2

4

5

bent, but this time in the opposite direction (Figure 4), in order to form the second branch. As training proceeds, the distances between the secondary branches should decrease. Once again, the bud closest to the bend will put forth a shoot that will become the next leader (Figure 5). This process continues until the tree has reached the desired height (Figure 6). From this point onwards, all new shoots should be pruned evenly.

Propagating a bonsai from cuttings

Most tropical and subtropical plants can be easily propagated from cuttings. Growing a bonsai by this method can

6

often take a whole year less than cultivating one from seed.

Cuttings are short sections of a plant, such as a stem with leaves, that are planted in a rooting medium where they put down roots and develop into an independent plant.

The advantage of using cuttings is that you are not dependent on flowers and the fruits that develop from them for propagating plants.

The following method has proved successful for propagating plants from cuttings. Fill a small flowerpot with potting compost, pressing it down lightly with the fingers. Remove the lower leaves from the cuttings and then, using a toothpick, drill holes into which the cuttings can be inserted. Cutting length should be between 5 and 7cm (2 and 3 in). Treating the cut with rooting

hormone will accelerate the rooting process. Once the cuttings have been inserted, water well and cover the flowerpot with a preserving jar or a plastic bag. Place the pot in a warm, dry place protected from direct sunlight.

Once the cuttings begin to root, gradually raise the jar or cut holes in the bag, starting with small ones and gradually making them bigger. A few weeks after rooting, you can start to feed the plants carefully. If the plants begin to outgrow the pot, carefully transplant them individually, cutting back the longest roots as you do so.

You can now begin to train the plants, using the methods with or without wire described above for seedlings.

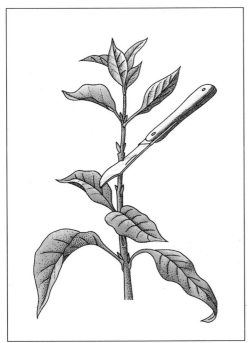

1. Cuttings are best taken from soft new growth, from which a short section should be cut immediately below a leaf node

2. Remove the lower leaves. Dip the cutting in rooting hormone to hasten the rooting process

Creating bonsais from young or pot plants

A lot of woody plants suitable for cultivation as indoor bonsais can be bought commercially as pot plants. These include, among others, several plants of the *Ficus* genus, such as *Ficus benjamina*.

Other trees can be purchased in specialist bonsai shops. These young plants have already been pruned several times in preparation for training as a bonsai.

If you use such plants as starting material, you will obtain a relatively sturdy bonsai rather more quickly than with the methods already outlined above.

In training them, however, you will have to take account of the restrictions already imposed by such characteristics as a predetermined trunk line. The trunk is usually so thick when you buy the plant that it is impossible to make any changes.

Training a pot plant

The most important criteria in buying a pot plant are the trunk line and the position of the larger secondary branches. The trunk should be thick at the base, so that with selective pruning it can be made to taper towards the apex. The position of the larger branches should match the desired shape or should be totally removed, since it is usually impossible to change their shape without leaving visible traces. Once you have selected a plant, take it out of its pot and

1. A Ficus benjamina *bought from a florist's shop serves as the basis for cultivating a bonsai in the upright style*

2. *Once all the extraneous branches have been removed, the remaining ones can be wired and trained to grow horizontally*

remove sufficient surface soil to reveal thick roots.

The point at which these thick roots strike out from the trunk is the point at which the trunk of the future bonsai will begin. The next step is to determine the height of the tree by removing the lower branches until you reach the one that is to be the lowest branch of the bonsai. Once the tree has been trained, this branch should, whenever possible, be the largest and sturdiest on the whole tree. Most people adopt the broom or upright style for their first bonsai (see page 15).

With the broom style, the main trunk is cut back to the point at which the first branch strikes out from the tree, allowing other branches of similar size to emerge from the same point. The upright style, on the other hand, requires a continuous

main trunk that tapers to the apex. Initial training involves the removal of branches so that, viewed from the front, those that remain emerge alternately from the left and right-hand sides of the trunk. The crown can be topped off at the rear by a few additional branches.

To make the tree appear a little older, the branches can be trained into a horizontal or even slightly drooping position. This requires the use of wire to train the branches to grow in the desired direction (see pages 30–1). The wire often has to be removed after four to six weeks so that it does not become ingrown. If the branches do not stay in the desired position, they will have to be wired again.

3. Once all the branches are growing in the desired direction, they can be cut back

4. About two weeks after pruning, the tree can be planted in a bonsai container

Seeds, cuttings or pot plants?

Species	Seeds	Cuttings	Pot plants
Arbutus unedo – strawberry tree	—	●	●
Bougainvillea glabra – Bougainvillea	—	●	+
Buddleia indica – Buddleia	—	●	—
Buxus harlandii – box	—	●	—
Camellia japonica – common camellia	—	●	+
Carmona microphylla – Fukien tea	●	●	—
Citrus – citrus trees	●	●	●
Crassula ovata – money plant	—	+	●
Cupressus macrocarpa 'Goldcrest' – Monterey cypress	—	—	+
Elaeagnus – elaeagnus, oleaster	●	●	●
Ficus benjamina – weeping fig	●	+	+
Ficus buxifolia – box-leaf fig	—	●	—
Ficus carica – common fig	●	●	●
Ficus microcarpa – laurel fig	●	+	●
Ficus natalensis – Natal fig	—	+	—
Ficus religiosa – bo tree, sacred fig tree	—	+	—
Ficus salicifolia – willow-leaved fig	—	+	●
Fuchsia – fuchsia	●	+	+
Haematoxylum campechianum – bloodwood tree	—	●	—
Hibiscus rosa-sinensis – rose of China	●	+	+
Lagerstroemia indica – crape myrtle	—	●	●
Lantana camara – yellow sage	●	●	+
Leptospermum scoparium – manuka, or New Zealand tea tree	●	●	+
Ligustrum japonicum – Japanese privet	●	●	—
Malpighia coccigera – miniature holly	—	●	●
Metrosideros excelsa – New Zealand Christmas tree	—	●	●
Murraya paniculata – orange jasmine	—	●	●
Myrciaria cauliflora – jaboticaba	—	●	—
Myrsine africana – myrsine	●	●	—
Myrtus communis – common myrtle	●	+	+
Nandina domestica – heavenly bamboo, sacred bamboo	—	●	●
Olea europaea – olive	●	●	+
Pinus halepensis – Aleppo pine	—	—	—*
Pinus pinea – umbrella or stone pine	●	—	●

Species	Seeds	Cuttings	Pot plants	
Pistacia lentiscus – mastic tree	—	●	●	
Podocarpus macrophyllus – Chinese podocarpus	—	●	●	
Portulacaria afra – purslane tree	—	+	+	
Punica granatum – pomegranate		+	+	+
Quercus ilex – evergreen oak, holm oak	●	—	—	
Quercus suber – cork oak	●	—	—	
Rosmarinus officinalis – common rosemary	—	●	+	
Sageretia thea – Sageretia	—	+	—	
Schefflera actinophylla – Queensland umbrella/octopus tree	—	+	+	
Serissa foetida – tree of a thousand stars	—	+	—	
Ulmus parvifolia – Chinese elm	—	+	●	

+ = preferred method
● = possible
— = difficult if not impossible

* Only obtainable as a bonsai!

The mechanics of bonsai

Even when a bonsai has reached its final shape, the plant will have to be constantly trained and shaped if it is to maintain its appearance. A specific set of tools is required for this, which will be described in this section. The photograph shows, from left to right, a pair of jin pliers for bending heavier gauge wire, two pairs of scissors or twig cutters for cutting smaller branches, a pair of concave branch cutters (bottom) and a pair of branch cutters for removing larger branches (top).

Branch pruning

One of the main reasons why a bonsai remains small is regular pruning. What should be cut back, and how far, depends on the plant and its current stage of development.

A young plant is generally allowed to develop longer shoots, so that it gains strength more quickly. It should be pruned in such a way that the lower branches remain longer.

1. Ficus salicifolia *before branch pruning*

2. *Each new shoot is cut back to between two and three leaves*

An assortment of tools

3. *The soil and drainage material should be changed immediately after hard pruning (see page 36)*

Older bonsais that have already been trained and shaped are pruned earlier and more frequently to encourage the development of a dense but dainty pattern of ramification.

Pruning also determines the direction in which a branch continues to grow, since a bud will erupt along the axis of the leaf closest to the cut. The new shoot will grow in approximately the same direction as the leaf is pointing. When training a pot plant, it is sometimes necessary to remove whole branches. This is done with a pair of special concave branch cutters, which can cut right up to the trunk of the tree to leave no snag at all. Such a clean cut will close up quickly and heal without leaving any visible marks.

Root pruning

Roots should always be pruned when a tree is repotted in order to maintain a balance between root mass and leaf mass. This is necessary because the roots have to supply the leaves with water and nutrients. However, the traffic is not all one way: the leaves also supply the roots

with nutrients and the energy produced by photosynthesis. A lack of balance between crown and roots usually shows itself only when the tree is under stress. If the roots, for example, are under-developed, then parts of the crown will dry out in hot weather, when the root-ball dries out temporarily. Conversely, if the roots are overdeveloped, then the crown cannot provide the roots with sufficient energy to sustain the metabolic process, particularly on overcast days or in shady locations. As a result, parts of the root system will die off, reducing the tree's ability to fight disease. It is then open to attack from fungi and bacteria and will eventually die.

If the roots are pruned regularly, a dense network of fine roots will form, mirroring the development of regularly pruned branches. This greatly increases the number of active root hairs. This type of root-ball is highly efficient and can supply even a thickly leafed crown with all the water and nutrients it requires for healthy growth.

Branch pruning determines the direction in which the new shoot will grow

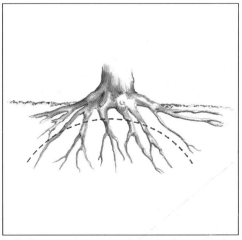

All the roots growing directly downwards from the trunk should be removed

Root pruning also affects the development of the aesthetically important surface roots. If the individual roots differ greatly in thickness, the thicker ones should be pruned severely. In this way, the weaker roots will gradually thicken.

Ideally, all the roots should be part of the surface root arrangement. This can be achieved by removing any roots growing straight downwards from the trunk, leaving only side roots. Since they alone will have to supply the tree with all the water and nutrients it requires, they will develop particularly quickly.

The best time to prune roots is in spring. However, most indoor bonsais can also be repotted and have their roots pruned at other times of the year, provided they are protected for the next two weeks from direct sunlight, strong draughts and a dry atmosphere.

Wiring

When a bonsai is being cultivated, the branches have to be trained to grow in a particular direction. In many cases, the direction of growth has to be altered radically. This can sometimes be achieved by selective pruning. Frequently, however, the only way of achieving a satisfactory result is to resort to wiring. Wire is wrapped round the branches that require training, both to bend them into the desired shape and to ensure they retain that shape once it has been achieved.

Aluminium wire, anodized or coloured brown to make it less conspicuous on the tree, has proved to be the best material for this technique. The wire must be relatively thick to train a branch to grow in the desired direction. Thicker wire will also not cut into the

1. The trunk should be wired first

2. The branches on the left and right-hand sides above are being trained with the same length of wire

3. To achieve a satisfying shape, secondary branches must also be wired

bark so easily. To avoid damaging the bonsai, it is essential to obey the following rules when wiring a tree:

- A tree should never be repotted while it is being wired.
- Start with the trunk or the larger branches and make sure these are fixed before going on to the thinner branches.
- Whenever possible, the same length of wire should be used to train two branches.
- If several lengths of wire are to be wrapped round the same branch, the lengths of wire should run parallel to each other.
- Lengths of wire should not cross over in such a way that a branch would be strangled if the wire were to become ingrown.

Suspended wiring

Particularly strong branches cannot be trained simply with wire. The wire would leave visible marks. Instead, suspended wiring is used.

To secure the suspended wiring, first attach a length of heavy gauge wire to the container by passing both ends through the drainage holes in the bottom. Tie a loop at either end just above the surface of the soil. Use thinner wire to guy the branches down. Where friction occurs, the limbs can be protected from damage with rubber tubing. Once the branch has been pulled into the desired position, the other end of the guy line can be attached to the loop of wire sticking out just above the surface of the soil (see diagram).

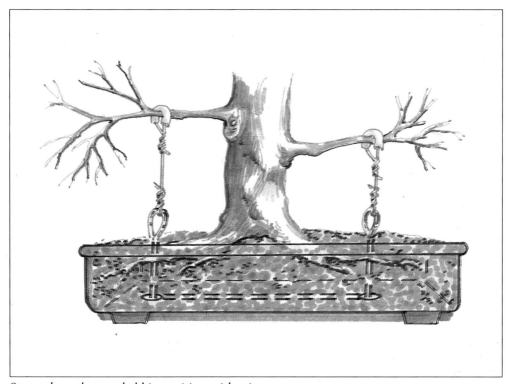

Strong branches are held in position with wires

Caring for your bonsai

Position

Since every indoor bonsai is a woody plant that grows outdoors in its native environment, it will thrive best in a location that comes as close as possible to the conditions it would encounter in its native habitat. The most important factors in determining those conditions are light, temperature, humidity, air flow, soil and the available water.

Light

Trees whose natural habitat is in the darker recesses of thick forests thrive even in low levels of light. However, such species seldom tolerate long periods of direct sunlight. These include, for example, *Schefflera actinophylla*. Such bonsais can be kept in windows that do not receive direct sunlight.

Most bonsais, however, need plenty of light. In their natural habitat, these trees form thick forests or stand magnificently in splendid isolation. Some are also grown as cultivated plants in plantations that thrive under a hot sun. As bonsais, therefore, they also need a bright, sunny position. For preference, this will be a window that receives the sun for at least one or two hours every day. However, when the sun is shining directly on a pane of glass, the area behind it becomes very hot. Even plants that need plenty of light should be protected from a blazing midday sun.

The distances between the leaves on new shoots indicate whether or not the plant is receiving sufficient light. For good development as a bonsai, the distances should be short. If the distances are too great, the plant needs more light. Either the plant should be moved to a lighter spot, or a grow lamp should be installed.

These lamps provide the exact amount of light required by the plant. They are available as normal lights or as fluorescent tubes. Mercury-vapour lamps are particularly effective but not cheap. Grow lamps can usually be purchased in normal lighting shops.

The specific light requirements of individual plant species are listed in "A–Z of indoor bonsai plants" (pages 48–107).

Temperature

House plants are classified into glasshouse plants and hothouse plants. These terms are also of relevance to indoor bonsais. Glasshouse plants come originally from subtropical regions and should be kept cool but frost-free in winter. The optimal temperature range is between 5 and 12°C (41 and 53°F). These conditions can be achieved only in an unheated conservatory or in a frost-free greenhouse. For most glasshouse plants, however, an unheated room, such as a bedroom, is perfectly adequate.

Hothouse plants are natives of the tropics and should be kept indoors all year round at temperatures between 18 and 24°C (64 and 75°F). Both glasshouse and hothouse plants can be put outdoors in summer, but if necessary must be allowed to accustom themselves gradually to unfiltered sunlight. Begin by putting them outside for short periods and then extend the time they spend out of doors by half an hour each day.

The warmer the position the plant is in, the more light it requires. As the temperature rises, the more water it will need.

Humidity

As noted above, most plants that can be kept all year round in heated living rooms come originally from tropical regions, where humidity is particularly high. In our homes, however, humidity is often very low, unless the room in question is not heated or there is an aquarium in it. A healthy atmosphere can be created by having plenty of

houseplants, which constantly release moisture into the room. Anyone not to wishing to resolve the humidity problem in this way, because of a feeling that the houseplants will put the bonsai "in the shade", can always install a humidifier.

The best possible conditions for the tree can be achieved by placing it in a large tray filled with water and hygroscopic pellets. The water evaporates, maintaining humidity levels within the optimal range.

Bonsais under a grow lamp

The more humid the atmosphere, the less water the tree uses. Conversely, if the air is particularly dry, the plant will require a great deal of water, since it gives off a lot of moisture into the atmosphere via its leaves. And, of course, a lot of moisture evaporates directly from the surface of the soil.

Air flow
Since the air flow in houses and flats is generally very sluggish, and the leaves of a bonsai can be very delicate, the plants therefore become easy prey for pests and diseases.

In the open air, the wind and weather ensure that trees develop suitably robust leaves. This affords them better protection from both excessive evaporation and pest infestation. For this reason alone, it is a good idea to keep bonsais out of doors for a time in the summer, either on a balcony or in the garden. If this is not possible, a fan placed near the plants and allowed to run for a few hours every day will have the same effect.

Soil

Many different types of naturally occurring soil are tolerated by most woody plants. Some plants, however, require quite specific soil conditions. The qualities of any particular soil are determined mainly by the materials of which it is made up, its pH value and its texture. Soil for bonsais generally consists of a particular combination of various materials.

Soil mixes for bonsais
Loam
Loam consists, among other things, of very fine particles of clay, has a great capacity for absorbing water, and combines readily with various other ingredients. These properties mean that loam has the ability to protect plants against major changes in soil conditions. Thus, for example, it can absorb excess water and release it slowly into the environment. Nutrients, particularly phosphates, are also absorbed and gradually made available to the plant.

Because of its fine, almost powdery structure, loam unfortunately compresses

A bonsai on a tray filled with hygroscopic pellets (F. benjamina)

From early summer to mid-autumn, indoor bonsais can be kept out of doors

very quickly. As a result, the small hollow spaces that are important in helping roots to breathe disappear. Because of this, fired clay particles imported from Japan, available under various brand names, are often added to bonsai soil. These particles maintain their coarse structure for one to two years, losing none of their positive buffering qualities during this time.

Sand

Sand also absorbs water through capillary action; unlike the water absorbed by loam, however, it is made available to the plant immediately. Sand also helps to keep the soil moist and to stabilize its crumb structure.

Lava

Lava contains trace elements and its numerous hollow spaces mean that air is trapped in the soil, which facilitates gas exchange and helps the roots to breathe. Lava can be bought in granular form.

Peat

Peat is organic matter, low in nutrients, which is cut from moors, bogs and fens. It is naturally acidic, but with the addition of lime its pH value can be adjusted to about 6 (slightly acidic) to make it a suitable medium for growing plants. Coarse-fibre peat is unsuitable for bonsai cultivation.

Some of the ingredients in a typical bonsai soil mix: coarse sand (top left), lava granules (top right), potting compost (bottom left), fired clay particles (bottom right)

Peat is used to make the soil more friable and to assist water retention. For environmental reasons, attempts have been made in recent years to dispense with peat cutting to protect the last few remaining moors. Most of the peat still available commercially has been imported from Russia. Not enough experiments have as yet been conducted with suitable alternatives. This is why peat is still a recommended ingredient in the soils for certain types of plants.

Potting compost

Compost usually consists of fine-fibred peat and sand, with a small amount of added nutrient material. It can also consist of other combinations of ingredients, such as bark, humus, peat and sand.

Azalea granulates

This grainy soil has a high water absorption capacity, while at the same time allowing excess water to drain away freely. The pH value is in the acidic range, i.e. lower than 7.

Planting a bonsai in its container

A plant potted for the first time in a bonsai container usually loses many of its roots. Provided that the leaves and branches are also pruned accordingly, most plants can lose up to two-thirds of their roots without coming to any harm. It is important that roots growing directly under the trunk should first be cut back or removed entirely. The lateral roots, on the other hand, should be retained. This makes the root-ball shallower so that it will fit more easily into a bonsai pot.

To prevent the soil falling out of the drainage holes in the container, cover them with fine plastic mesh, held on with wire. Then put a layer of coarse, granular material – usually fired clay particles – into the bottom of the container and place the plant on top. Now fill the container to the half-way point with fired clay particles, ensuring no empty spaces are left in between the roots by pressing the particles into all the nooks and crannies with a piece of wood. Then fill the container up with a mixture of equal parts of clay particles, sand and peat. The particular soil requirements of individual plant species are outlined in more detail in "A–Z of indoor bonsai species" (pages 48–107).

Press the soil down lightly and then water generously. Do not begin to feed the plant until at least two weeks after potting up.

Changing the soil

If the plant has been in the same soil for more than two years, then it is time the soil was changed. The same applies to indoor bonsais that have been watered very frequently, particularly with ordinary tap water. Frequent watering leads to a sharp increase in the soil's salt content, making it necessary to change the soil after just a year.

When the plant is repotted, the root-ball should be only slightly moist. Begin by removing the plant from the container and loosening the root-ball slightly by pressing it lightly from the side. Then pull the roots apart and remove about two-thirds of the soil. Those roots growing directly down from the trunk should be severely pruned or removed altogether.

The next step is to prune the side roots, with the sturdier ones being cut back more severely than thinner ones. This will make the side roots grow even more. Next, replace the plastic mesh

1. *The root-ball can be removed easily from the container*

2. *Use a root hook to separate the roots carefully from each other*

3. *Now the roots can be pruned easily*

covering the drainage holes with new pieces of the same material – by this time they are usually blocked with chalky deposits. Place some drainage material in the container, put the plant on top of it, fill the pot up to the half-way point with clay particles, and then add the soil. Press it down lightly and water generously once.

After about two weeks, you can begin to feed the plant. The best time for changing the soil is in spring. Most tropical and subtropical plants can even be repotted between late winter and mid-spring.

4. *Use a brush to expose the surface roots*

5. *Cover the drainage holes in the container with plastic mesh*

Watering

As everyone knows, the amounts and duration of rainfall vary widely across the globe. Plants from regions of high rainfall usually require more water as bonsais than those from drier regions. Thus a *Carmona microphylla* (Fukien tea) should never be allowed to dry out

6. *To make the soil free draining, the first layer should consist of fired clay particles*

7. *Place the tree on top of the clay particles and fill the container with the rest of the soil mix*

completely, while a *Portulacaria afra* (money or jade plant) will survive for several weeks without any water at all. Conversely, the roots of the jade plant rot if watered every day, although this is precisely the right treatment on most days for the Fukien tea.

If you are uncertain as to what any particular bonsai needs in the way of water, a useful rule of thumb is to water the plant whenever the soil surface has dried out slightly. In this way, the plant will receive water until the moisture stored in the soil has been used up.

In the following circumstances, frequent watering is necessary irrespective of the type of plant:

- the plant has a lot of large leaves;
- the bonsai has not been repotted for a long time;
- the container is too small;
- the container is extremely shallow with a large soil surface area; and/or
- the room is well heated.

If the soil surface, for example, dries out again within a day, it may be that replacing the soil or putting the plant in a larger container will eliminate the need for frequent watering.

To pour or to immerse?
Basically, watering should be as simple as possible. However, if the water is poured from above in the normal way, the salts dissolved in the water accumulate in the soil, causing root damage and preventing the plant from absorbing water properly. If rainwater is available, the risk of salt accumulation is much reduced.

The advantage of pouring the water on from above is that it takes little effort, the soil can be kept evenly moist, and there is no risk of excess water accumulation. The disadvantage is that the plants must be watered relatively frequently and very regularly.

Another possible way of supplying a bonsai with water is to immerse it briefly. The entire container is plunged into water up to the point at which the surface roots strike out from the trunk. It is kept immersed until there are no more air bubbles rising to the surface. With this method, the risk of salts accumulating in the soil is very low, since much of the excess water drains away immediately after immersion through the holes in the bottom of the container, taking most of the salts with it. Unfortunately, this also applies to the salts that provide nutrition, so the plant must be fed more frequently. Another disadvantage is that the plant gets very wet. With high containers, therefore, the plant must have plenty of well-established roots. The air temperature must also be high enough for the excess moisture to be used up immediately, so that it can be reduced to a healthy level very quickly.

A mixture of the two methods can be particularly successful. The plant can be immersed once a week or at even longer intervals, with normal watering taking place whenever the soil surface is slightly dry. In this way, the advantages of the two watering methods can be combined, thus minimizing the disadvantage.

Immerse the bonsai container in the water for just a few seconds

Use a 'watering bulb' to distribute the water evenly

Water quality

Water quality has a significant influence on the health of a plant. To make it easier for you to choose the right kind for your bonsai, the properties of various types of water are outlined below.

Rainwater

Most plants will thrive perfectly well on rainwater. It contains few salts and is very soft. The best way of collecting rainwater is to take it from guttering. Builders' merchants sell devices that can be fitted to downpipes to control the flow of water, the water being fed into a water butt. At the beginning of a downpour, the water contains relatively large quantities of harmful substances and is fairly acidic. For this reason, water should not be fed into the butt until it has been raining for some time, and most of the harmful substances in the air have already fallen to earth.

If plants are supplied solely with rainwater, they should be fed a little extra lime.

Tap water

Tap water varies widely from region to region. Its relative hardness or softness

Carmona microphylla *should never be allowed to dry out completely*

depends on the way in which it is obtained. Thus water taken from reservoirs created by damming a river valley can be very soft. Water filtered through river banks, on the other hand, often has high levels of calcium and other mineral salts. Your local water company will be able to provide you with the relevant values for the water supplied to your home.

Plants that require an acidic growing medium, that is one with a low pH value (less than 7), should not be watered with hard water, i.e. water with a high proportion of mineral salts, since it tends to have a higher pH level.

Hardness caused by calcium salts can be reduced by boiling the water or leaving it to stand, although this will have only a modest effect on any other mineral salts that may be present. The proportion of such salts in tap water also varies widely, but is almost always several times greater than in rainwater. Because of this, plants should be watered in such a way that these salts do not accumulate in the soil. You can either immerse them at regular intervals or always pour on so much water that most of it drains away.

Portulacaria afra *will survive for some time without water*

Distilled and de-ionized water

The proportion of salts in the water you use for your plants can be reduced slightly by blending it with distilled or de-ionized water. If you use equal proportions of both kinds of water, the salt content will be reduced by half. If you use distilled water only, which has very little buffering capacity, the pH value of the soil may be changed very rapidly and very considerably, which may cause great damage to the plants.

Well water

Some people have a supply of groundwater from a well. However, such water should be examined thoroughly before using it to supply plants. The mineral salt content of groundwater is often so high that it will damage them.

It is clear from this that rainwater is best suited to indoor bonsais. To prevent too sharp a decline in the lime content of the soil, which is important for micro-organisms, the rainwater can be supplemented at regular intervals with harder tap water.

If only hard tap water is available, you should not try to cultivate plants that require soil with a low pH value. Such plants will be very well served by soft tap water.

If you use tap water for your plants, two-thirds of the soil should be replaced every year.

Feeding

Even compared with a normal houseplant, an indoor bonsai has to make do with a small amount of soil. It must therefore be fed properly if it is to remain healthy. The following types of fertilizer are available commercially.

Inorganic fertilizers

An inorganic fertilizer provides a plant with nutrients in the form of salts. In the case of liquid fertilizers, these salts are in solution in water. Inorganic fertilizers are immediately absorbed by the plant but raise the mineral salt content of the soil. Since the soil in what are usually very small containers is very sensitive to change, great care must be exercised in the use of inorganic fertilizers. If anything, the recommended fertilizer strength should be reduced slightly.

Slow-release fertilizers

If you have difficulty in keeping to a regular plant-feeding schedule, you should consider using slow-release fertilizers, which provide plants with a balanced level of nutrients over a long period. One application can last several months. However, there is still the risk of inaccurate doses.

Organic fertilizers

With organic fertilizers, the nutrients are part of an organic substance and are not available to the plant until that substance has been broken down in the soil by

Nitrogen deficiency

micro-organisms. This happens so slowly that the plant immediately absorbs the nutrients as they are released. There is no risk of salts accumulating. Such fertilizers are kinder to plants, but require some time and a soil rich in the relevant micro-organisms to take effect.

Regular feeding will ensure that a plant receives an adequate supply of the main nutrients it needs: nitrogen, phosphorous and potassium. In addition, many fertilizers contain trace elements such as boron, copper and manganese. Since inappropriate use of fertilizers can damage plants, the following rules should be observed:

- Never add fertilizer to dry soil. Ideally, a plant should be watered generously before being fed.
- Use inorganic fertilizers in lower concentrations than suggested in the manufacturer's instructions. Feed plants more frequently to compensate for the lower doses.
- If you apply too much fertilizer by mistake, it is a good idea to rinse the root ball thoroughly with water.
- Newly repotted plants should not be

fed for at least two weeks, since the new soil will have adequate reserves of nutrients.
- Plants should be fed more sparingly in winter, since most of them are virtually inactive during the darker months.
- Plants that have been badly starved of nutrients should always be fed with liquid fertilizers.

In addition to these general rules, the particular requirements of individual plants should also be taken into account (see "A–Z of indoor bonsai species"). If a plant is suffering from a deficiency of trace elements, this can be remedied by special preparations available in specialist shops. It is also worth repeating that excessive feeding can also be harmful to plants. For example, if plants are watered regularly with hard tap water, they should be fed with a fertilizer that contains no lime.

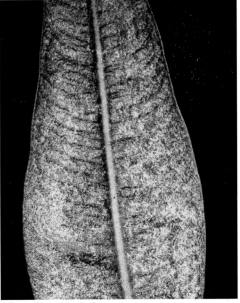

Potassium deficiency

Phosphorous deficiency

Typical deficiency symptoms	
Nutrients	Symptoms
Nitrogen (N)	poor growth, lack of flowers, leaves sometimes tinged with red
Phosphorous (P)	low resistance to disease and frost, brown to yellowish leaf margins, whole leaves die off
Potassium (K)	poor growth, susceptibility to disease, new shoots turn yellow
Calcium (Ca)	older leaves turn yellowish while the veins remain green (chlorosis)
Magnesium (Mg)	new shoots turn yellow and die
Boron (B)	leaf tips turn white
Copper (Cu)	irregular brown spots on leaves
Manganese (Ma)	new shoots turn light yellow
Iron (Fe)	new leaves are misshapen and yellowish
Molybdenum (Mo)	poor growth, leaves turn light yellow

Pests and diseases

Since indoor bonsais are not being kept in their natural habitat, they are particularly susceptible to pest infestation. There are certain pests that attack only particular plants and others that can occur on virtually any plant.

Pest control by chemical means is a problem inside houses and flats, since the toxic substances employed are harmful to human beings as well. If control without chemicals proves impossible, any treatment should be carried out in the summer, outdoors.

Whitefly

The larvae of these small white insects suck on plants. In doing so, they give off a sticky substance on which the fungus that causes sooty mould grows. As it grows, the fungus deprives the plant of light. The mature females lay a few eggs every day over a certain period, which means that every day a few new creatures

hatch out, making control more difficult. Insecticides often kill off only the mature adults. Yellow whitefly-traps have proved effective. The insects are attracted by the yellow colour of the traps and when they land on them they stick to the birdlime with which they are coated. It is also possible to buy a parasitic ichneumon fly that lays its eggs in the whitefly larvae, which then serve as food for the young flies. Species that are particularly susceptible to whitefly infestation include sageretia (*Sageretia theezans*), pomegranates (*Punica granatum*), fuchsias (*Fuchsia*) and hibiscus (*Hibiscus rosa-sinensis*). However, other species are far from immune.

Spider mites

These tiny arachnids, which are very difficult to see, suck at the plant throughout several larval stages. The foliage turns a dull, mottled, yellowish-green colour. Easier to detect are the old skins shed each time the larvae moult, which appear as small white dots on the undersides of the leaves. Some plants are able to tolerate a certain degree of spider

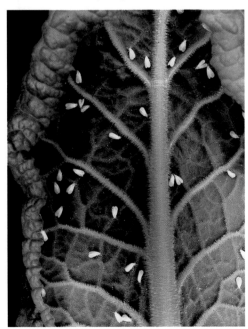

Whitefly

Spider mites

45

mite infestation and adapt accordingly. Several varieties of the *Ficus* genus belong to this category, including the weeping fig (*Ficus benjamina*). Other species lose their entire foliage in no time at all. If the new growth also becomes infested and dies off, then there is very little that can be done to save the plant.

Most of the commercially available sprays are active only against mature adults. Certain larval stages and the eggs remain unharmed. This makes it necessary to repeat the treatment several times. It is also possible to introduce predatory mites into the room. They will attack and eat the plant-eating mites without doing any damage to the bonsais. Such predatory mites can be bought in specialist shops.

Chinese elms (*Ulmus pavifolia*) and many of the *Ficus* varieties are particularly susceptible to spider mite infestation. In many cases, the mites then move on to attack other species.

Scale insects

Scale insects are also tiny, sap-sucking insects that feed on the plant as they pass through several larval, mostly immobile stages. They are protected by a flattened, waxy covering. The only way of detecting scale insects in the initial stage is through their sticky secretion. Scale insects prefer *Ficus* varieties and myrtles. Infestation can be kept in check by regularly removing the insects from the plant. In cases of heavy infestation, chemical treatment should be left to a specialist.

Mealy bugs

Mealy bugs are easily recognized by their white, waxy excretion that looks like cotton wool. If the infestation is not too heavy, they can be removed from the plant by hand.

If an insecticide is to be used, a wetting agent must be added to it, since the insects will otherwise be protected by their waxy excretion, which repels water. Mealy bug infestation is not particularly

Scale insects

Mealy bugs

common, but occurs regularly on virtually all species of plant.

Greenfly

Sap-sucking greenfly are particularly likely to attack Fukien tea (*Carmona microphylla*), pomegranates (*Punica granatum*) and the sageretias (*Sageretia theezans*), but many other plants are also susceptible. In the initial stage, before any eggs have been laid, they can be flushed away by a strong jet of water. At later stages, plants can be treated with an insecticide that is active against sap-sucking insects.

Fungi

When conditions are unfavourable, indoor bonsais can be attacked by various destructive fungi. Some of the signs of attack are brown leaf tips, a white coating on foliage, and blackened tips on new shoots. If you suspect a plant has succumbed to a fungus, you should seek advice in a specialist bonsai shop.

Greenfly

Sooty mould

Powdery mildew

A–Z of indoor bonsai species

The entries on individual species, which are listed alphabetically by their Latin name, all follow the same pattern. The botanical and common names are followed by a brief description of the tree or shrub. Some indoor bonsais bear fruit from time to time. Even if the fruit is normally edible (as with various citrus fruits, for example), you are advised not to eat any fruit produced by bonsais, since you can never be certain that the plant was not treated with harmful chemicals before being sold.

   The description of each species concludes with a note on any particular features that make it suitable for training as a bonsai. To make it easier to find, the following information is presented under the headings as explained below:

Position: recommended light level, temperature, and any seasonal changes that may be necessary. The recommended light level is also listed at the beginning of each entry: ● = shade, ◐ = partial shade, ○ = bright to full sun.

Soil: exact details of the ideal soil mix. The soil is normally changed every two years. Any exceptions to this general rule are always noted.

Watering: how often should the tree or shrub be watered, and what kind of water best suits it? Do the requirements change with the seasons?

Feeding: details of appropriate fertilizers and the correct feeding schedule.

Training: possible styles, tips on wiring, suspended wiring and pruning.

Acquiring a plant: what is the best way of getting started – with seeds, cuttings or a pot plant?

Pests: a list of all the pests to which the plant is particularly susceptible.

Arbutus unedo
Killarney strawberry tree   ○ – ◐

The Killarney strawberry tree is found mainly in Mediterranean regions, where it forms large bushes or even small trees. Its trunk develops a deep-brown bark and a gnarled appearance when old. The rough branches bear alternately spaced, smooth, leathery serrated leaves about the size of an oak leaf. The flowers, similar in appearance to lily-of-the-valley, emerge in clusters in autumn and develop into round, red fruits with a coarse skin that look rather like strawberries. In Portugal, the edible fruits are used to make a liqueur.

   Because of its large leaves, the plant should be able to reach a minimum height of 50cm (20in). As a result, it is seldom cultivated as a bonsai.

Position: partial shade to full sun all year round. *Ar. unedo* should be placed outdoors in summer. During the winter, it can be kept in a frost-free but cool position, or in an unheated room.
Soil: a mixture of three parts fired clay particles, two parts sand and one part potting compost. With young plants, two-thirds of this mixture should be replaced every two years. If fed regularly, older plants will survive

Arbutus unedo, *young plant*

happily for longer in the same soil.
Watering: keep evenly moist with
ordinary tap water. When the weather is
hot, the tree will require plenty of water.
However, it will usually tolerate being
dry for short periods. If it is kept
indoors in winter, it should be kept
moist. To determine the correct watering
schedule, keep an eye on the soil surface.
If it is only slightly moist or even dry,
then the plant can be watered again.
Feeding: during the growing season, feed
every two weeks with an organic
fertilizer. The tree should not be fed if it
is kept at temperatures of less than 12^0C
(53^0F) in winter. If it is kept indoors in
an unheated room in winter, then it
should be fed every four weeks.
Training: the most popular styles are the
upright and broom styles. Attempts to
train the tree in other styles will not
succeed unless the training begins very
early or the trunk starts by chance to
grow in a different direction. With
young plants, trim new shoots back to
one to three sets of leaves once the shoot

has reached a length of about 20cm
(8in). If the leaves are widely spaced,
leave just one leaf on shoots in the outer
crown area.

The wounds caused by removing
larger branches should be treated
immediately with wound sealant to
promote swift healing.

Generally speaking, only one-year-old
branches can be wired without leaving
visible marks on the bark. Older
branches tend to be very brittle and stiff.
The only way of shaping these older
branches is by guying them down with
suspended wiring.

Acquiring a plant: propagation from
cuttings is possible. Pot plants, often
very large ones, can sometimes be bought
in garden centres or florists shops.
Specialist bonsai shops do not stock
Killarney strawberry trees, so if you want
to cultivate one as a bonsai, you will
have to do it yourself.

Pests: Killarney strawberry trees trained
as bonsais do not seem to be particularly
susceptible to any pests.

49

Bougainvillea glabra
Bougainvillea, or paper flower   ○

This plant, now found all over the tropics as a shrub or scrambling climber, originally comes from Brazil. The trunk of older plants is light beige in colour. The pointed, smooth-edged, green leaves are arranged alternately. At the beginning of the flowering period, the terminal leaves turn purple or reddish-orange and, arranged in groups of three, form the envelope for the emergent flower. There are now many differently coloured varieties.

Since bougainvilleas are climbers, it is difficult both to shape them and to cultivate them for their flowers.

Position: bright and sunny. In summer, the plant will flourish better outdoors than inside. In winter, it is best kept in a cool, unheated room. If the plant is to flower, it should be kept in an even colder but frost-free place where it will usually shed its leaves and put out new shoots in spring. It will also flower if the weather is sunny and warm.
Soil: a mix of two parts fired clay particles, one part sand and one part potting compost. Other well-draining soil mixes are also possible.
Watering: plenty of water is needed when the plant is putting out new shoots in spring, but always adjust the water supply to the plant's needs, giving more on warm days and less when the weather is cooler. In winter, particularly when the plant has shed its leaves, do not water until the soil surface has dried out. Tap water is quite suitable.
Feeding: every two weeks from early spring to late summer with an organic fertilizer. Do not feed in winter.

Bougainvillea glabra, *young plant*

Training: all styles are feasible, with no one style being easier to achieve than any other. In the early years, when the plant is acquiring its definitive shape, the flowers should be relegated to the background. The tendrils can grow very vigorously and should be cut back severely to encourage them to grow thicker. Only the first section of each new shoot should be wired. The rest should be allowed to grow freely before being cut back. Pruning should take place once the shoots have reached a length of between 30 and 40cm (12 and 16in). Depending on the branch's position in the crown, trim back to between one to five leaves. Older trees can be trimmed back once the new shoots are about 10cm (4in) in length. Older branches usually have to be trained with suspended wiring.
Acquiring a plant: can be propagated from cuttings. Young plants can also be bought in florists shops and garden centres.
Pests: dry air in centrally heated homes encourages spider mite infestation.

Buddleja indica, *after its first pruning*

Buddleja indica
Buddleia   ○

This evergreen shrub (also known as *Nicodemia diversifolia*), a native of Madagascar, bears its leaves in opposite pairs; with their slight indentations, they resemble oak leaves. The tiny yellowish flowers are arranged in small clusters.

This is a relatively undemanding plant, and will be quite happy in rooms with frequent changes of temperature. It is not yet widely cultivated as a bonsai.

Position: bright, can be exposed to the sun for hours at a time. However, direct midday sun should be avoided. The plant can be kept outdoors in summer. In winter, it is best kept in a cool, unheated room, although it will also survive in a room that is heated during the day but cools down at night.

Soil: a mix of equal parts of fired clay particles, sand and potting compost. Two-thirds of the soil should be replaced every two years, with the roots being pruned at the same time.

Watering: tap water is quite suitable. Frequent watering is necessary on hot summer days. Water as soon as the soil surface is slightly dry. Water less frequently in winter if the plant is in a cool location.

Feeding: every two weeks during the growing season with an organic fertilizer. In winter, feeding at intervals of four to six weeks is quite sufficient.

Training: because of the size of the leaves, the tree really needs to be at least 30cm (12in) in height. Training must begin at an early stage because older plants are difficult to shape. With selective pruning, the plant can be trimmed into the broom or upright styles. To create a cascade bonsai, you will have to wire the branches, or use suspended wiring. One-year-old twigs can be easily wired. Older branches will have to be guyed down with suspended wiring. With young plants that are still developing, new shoots should be cut back as soon as they are 10–20cm (4–8in) in length. With older, more mature specimens, pruning can be done at an earlier stage, which encourages twiggy growth.

Acquiring a plant: *B. indica* can be propagated from cuttings. Potted specimens can sometimes be bought in florists shops or garden centres. They are also occasionally available as bonsais in specialist shops.

Pests: *B. indica* is quite susceptible to whitefly infestation.

Buxus harlandii
Box ○

This evergreen shrub, with its small, lanceolate leaves, is a native of China. It has a corky, deeply furrowed trunk, light beige in colour. The yellowish-green flowers are inconspicuous but develop in large numbers.

Only a few specimens survive long indoors, and only experienced bonsai growers seem able to keep this plant for long periods. So beginners should steer clear!

Position: a bright, sunny, indoor spot. Box can also be put outdoors in summer. In winter, it is best kept in a cool, unheated room, with a temperature of between 5 and 18°C (41 and 64°F).
Soil: a mix of three parts fired clay particles, one part sand and one part potting compost. The soil should not be acidic (acid soil has a pH value of less than 7).
Watering: use hard tap water. On warm summer days, boxes need a lot of water. It is important that the soil should not be allowed to dry out completely. Less water is required in winter, when the soil surface can be allowed to dry out slightly before watering. The cooler its position, the less water the plant needs.
Feeding: every two weeks from spring to late summer with an organic fertilizer. One feed is sufficient in winter.
Training: boxes can be trimmed into any style of bonsai. Extreme styles, such as the cascade, must be started at an early stage, since older trunks cannot be bent into shape without damaging the bark. One to two-year-old branches can be wired. Older branches will have to be guyed down with suspended wiring.

Once they are 10cm (4in) long, new shoots should be cut back to a length of 1–2cm ($^{1}/_{2}$–1in).
Acquiring a plant: boxes are easily propagated from cuttings. Young plants are not readily available commercially. Boxes are widely available as finished bonsais, or can be ordered from specialist shops.
Pests: *B. harlandii* is not susceptible to attack from pests.

Camellia japonica
Common camellia ○ – ◑

This plant, which occurs as a large shrub and a tree in its native Japan and Korea, has a beautiful, smooth stem or trunk. The tough textured leaves, shiny on top, are arranged alternately on the light-brown branches. The large flowers develop from sturdy buds in early spring. There are many cultivars bearing flowers of different colours, shapes, and sizes.

The small-leaved varieties and hybrids, such as 'Cornish Snow' or 'Cornish Spring', are particularly suitable for cultivation as bonsais. Camellias lose their buds if they are exposed to drastic changes in their environment, such as a drop in humidity in centrally heated rooms in winter.

Position: in summer, a light, partially shaded but warm spot, in the open air if at all possible. Plants should be brought indoors before the first autumn frosts. In winter, they are best kept in a cool position where the humidity is not too low. Camellias can also spend the winter out of doors in a sheltered, frost-free location.
Soil: must be acidic (pH of 5.5). A mix of two parts peaty soil, one part sand and one part fired clay particles is

Buxus harlandii, *about fifteen years old*

Camellia japonica, *about fifteen years old*

suitable. Other acidic soil mixes, such as the azalea soil used in Japan, could also be used. With young plants, the soil should be changed every two years; with older ones, change half the soil every three to five years.

Watering: rainwater is to be preferred. Camellias should be kept moist in summer, but require less water in winter.

Feeding: every two weeks with an organic fertilizer once the flowers have appeared. Camellias should be fed for the last time in early summer, to encourage bud formation.

Training: camellias often react unpredictably to pruning and wiring, so it is best to proceed with caution. They can be trimmed easily into the upright style. Because of the large leaves, the minimum height should be 40cm (16in). One-year-old shoots should be wired carefully and not too tightly. Older branches will have to be guyed down. Depending on the stage of development and the planned size of the plant, new shoots that develop in spring after the flowering period can be cut back to one to three leaves once they have reached a length of 10–20cm (4–8in). In the case of an older plant, training is best started in spring. Large cuts will then knit together quickly if treated properly.

Acquiring a plant: the propagation of camellias requires a little experience. If you want to train a camellia as a bonsai, it is best to buy one of the wide range of varieties available in florists shops or garden centres.

Camellias already cultivated as bonsais are only seldom available commercially, and even then they are usually still very young.

Pests: camellias are not very susceptible to pest infestation.

Carmona microphylla
Fukien tea ◑

The Fukien tea, which takes its name from the eponymous Chinese province, is a native of Asia. Its correct botanical name is *Ehretia buxifolia*, but it is much better known by the synonym *Carmona microphylla*. This evergreen shrub, whose bark has an irregular surface that imparts the appearance of great age after just a few years, has small, glossy leaves arranged in alternate groups of four, with three lobes at the tips and short, sturdy, light-coloured hairs on the underside. The small white flowers may give way to red, inedible berries.

Two varieties are available commercially: the small-leaved *C. microphylla*, usually sold only as a young plant, and the larger-leaved *C. macrophylla*, which has often already developed a thicker trunk. The latter is the more robust, and therefore to be preferred.

Position: needs to be kept in a warm spot all year round. In summer, the Fukien tea can be placed in a partially shaded place outside. In winter, when central heating sharply reduces humidity levels indoors, the plant should be placed on a tray filled with small hygroscopic pellets and water. The bonsai container should be placed on the hygroscopic pellets in such a way that the soil is not in direct contact with the water. The water should be topped up regularly.

Soil: most plants are imported from China in very loamy soil. Watering very quickly compresses the soil, so that the roots are no longer receiving sufficient oxygen. For this reason, the loamy soil must be changed as soon as possible. Since the Fukien tea is very sensitive to any reduction in its root mass, the soil change should take place in stages. The replacement growing medium should consist of fired clay particles, which are similar in composition to the loamy soil in which the plants are usually imported. Unlike this soil, however, the fired particles retain their granular structure for a relatively long time. When the plant is well established, it can be transplanted to a soil mix containing equal parts of fired clay particles, sand and potting compost. The soil is best changed in spring.

Young plants need to have their soil changed every two years, whereas older bonsais can be repotted less frequently, provided they have been watered with rainwater.

Watering: keep as evenly moist as possible. Rainwater is to be preferred, otherwise use tap water that has been left to stand for a good while. If you forget to water the plant and the root-ball dries out totally, you can usually kiss goodbye to your Fukien tea.

Feeding: every two weeks from spring to autumn with an organic fertilizer, and every four weeks in winter.

Training: a Fukien tea can be trimmed into any of the Japanese bonsai styles. One- to two-year-old branches can be trained by wiring. Thicker branches will have to be guyed down with suspended wiring in order to avoid damage to the bark. In many cases, the larger-leaved variety has already acquired a definite shape when you buy it, which has to be maintained or completed. The smaller-leaved variety, on the other hand, is usually just spherical and is seldom sold ready trimmed into a particular shape. Such a plant requires more drastic surgery. Training can be spread over the whole year. The only proviso is that the plant should not have been recently

Carmona microphylla, *about fifteen years old, Rüger collection*

repotted. Depending on the plant's stage of development, the very stiff new shoots should be cut back from a length of between 10 and 20cm (4 and 8in) to between one and three clusters of leaves. If older branches have to be removed, the cuts should be properly sealed in order that the wounds heal up quickly.

Acquiring a plant: the Fukien tea is one of the plants most frequently sold for cultivation as a bonsai. It can even be bought frequently in do-it-yourself stores and fairs. It can also be propagated easily from cuttings or from seed.
Pests: the Fukien tea is a favourite plant of various species of aphid.

Citrus
Citrus trees   ○

There are about sixty species of citrus tree that are found in all the subtropical regions of the world, where they have been cultivated for centuries for their edible fruits. Most of them are evergreen shrubs or small trees, whose prickly branches carry alternate, egg-shaped leaves. The white flowers appear on young branches and then develop into the various kinds of citrus fruit.

Since the leaves are relatively large, a citrus bonsai should ideally be at least 50cm (20 in) height. Only those varieties bearing small fruit are suitable if you wish to incorporate the fruit into the design.

Position: a bright, sunny spot all year round. In summer, citrus trees flourish particularly well in the garden or on a balcony. In winter, they should be kept inside, in a well-lit position in an unheated room. A conservatory or greenhouse would also make a suitable winter home, although only if they are frost-free.

Soil: slightly acidic (pH lower than 7). A mix of two parts Japanese azalea granules, one part fired clay particles, one part sand and one part potting compost would be suitable. Half the soil should be renewed every two to three years. The roots should always be pruned when the soil is changed.

Watering: rainwater is to be preferred. In summer, citrus trees need a lot of water. In the winter, on the other hand, the root-ball should be kept just slightly moist. A good rule of thumb is that the colder its position, the less water the tree needs.

Feeding: every two weeks from spring to autumn with an organic fertilizer. A citrus tree should not be fed during the winter.

Training: a citrus tree can be trimmed into any of the standard styles, provided training starts early enough. Older trunks or branches cannot easily be persuaded to change their shape or direction. A young tree can even be trimmed into the broom style without wiring.

Should the tree start to take on a different shape, it will have to be wired or guyed down. One-year-old branches can be wired. Older branches will have to be guyed down to avoid damaging the bark. Once new shoots have reached a length of 10–20cm (4–8in), they should be cut back to one to three leaves.

Acquiring a plant: citrus trees can be propagated by sowing the appropriate seeds or pips. However, plants propagated in this way will not flower for many years.

Dwarf or ornamental orange trees can be bought in florists shops or garden centres; their small fruit makes them quite suitable for cultivation as a bonsai. Citrus trees are only seldom sold as finished bonsais. Such trees are usually grafts.

Pests: if a citrus tree is kept in too warm and too dry a place in winter, it is likely to be attacked by spider mites. Citrus trees are also quite susceptible to scale insect infestation.

Citrus, *about eight years old*

Crassula ovata
Money or jade plant ○

This succulent shrub is a native of South Africa and has opposite, rounded, fleshy leaves. The sturdy branches are very evenly distributed along the length of the thick trunk, which becomes very gnarled with age. Small, star-shaped, white or pale pink flowers adorn the new shoots in the spring.

Its tree-like appearance makes this plant a very good choice for cultivation as a bonsai, and since it is relatively undemanding it can even be recommended to beginners. It is often confused with *Portulacaria afra*.

Position: bright, if possible with direct sunlight. In summer, *C. ovata* can also be kept out of doors. Since it will not tolerate frost, it must be brought indoors in winter and placed in a cool room.
Soil: a mix of three parts fired clay particles, two parts sand and one part potting compost. Most of the soil should be changed every two to three years.
Watering: the plant should be kept evenly moist in summer. However, it will not come to too much harm if it dries out a little. In winter, it should always be a little drier. Normal tap water is quite suitable.
Feeding: every three to four weeks from spring to autumn with a fertilizer low in nitrogen (e.g. one suitable for cacti). Do not feed in winter.
Training: the branches are naturally very evenly arranged, which makes it somewhat boring as a bonsai. It is best to break up this regularity by removing some of the branches. Young branches can be trained by wiring. However, the wire can easily become ingrown, since the branches thicken very rapidly at certain times.

New shoots can be trimmed back once they have reached a length of 5–10cm (2–4in). In deciding how far to cut back, take the desired height of the branch as a guideline. Depending on the branch's position in the crown, leave between one and three pairs of leaves intact.
Acquiring a plant: *C. ovata* can be easily propagated from cuttings. Leave the cuts to dry up for a few hours and then plant the cuttings straight into the potting compost. The plant is often sold in garden centres and florists shops as a pot plant. You may occasionally have the chance to acquire a well-established houseplant, which you can use as material for creating a bonsai. Such specimens have usually not been trained, but simply cut back.
Pests: *C. ovata* is susceptible to attack by mealy bugs.

Crassula ovata, *still developing*

Cupressus macrocarpa 'Goldcrest'
Monterey cypress　　　　　　　○

Cypresses are conifers that have small, scaly, densely packed needles. *C. macrocarpa* is a native of North America. When young, it is broadly columnar in its habit or growth pattern. As it grows older and its branches get heavier, it becomes broad crowned. *C. macrocarpa* is one of the few cypresses that can be kept indoors. It is not suitable for beginners; nevertheless, under the right conditions it will flourish without any special treatment. 'Goldcrest' is the variety most widely available commercially, and is easily recognized by its greenish-yellow foliage.

Position: light and sunny. The Monterey cypress is best kept out of doors in summer. In winter, put it by the window in an unheated room. It will even tolerate being in a heated room where the temperature is over 18°C (64°F), provided that the humidity level does not fall below 50%.
Soil: a mix of one part fired clay particles, two parts sand and one part potting compost. Two-thirds of the soil should be changed every two years.
Watering: keep evenly moist. The tree is equally tolerant of temporary dryness and occasional over-watering. Tap water is quite satisfactory.
Feeding: every two weeks from early spring to autumn with an organic or organic fertilizer. In winter, monthly feeds will be sufficient.
Training: in theory, the Monterey cypress can be trained into all styles, although the upright style is the one most commonly adopted. The only styles that can be readily achieved without the use of wire are the broom style, which is uncharacteristic of cypresses, or the columnar form that is characteristic of younger specimens. For other styles, you will have to resort to wiring. Cypress branches are long and flexible. If guyed down to a wire threaded through the container, they are likely to be torn from the trunk, so great care must be exercised in the use of suspended wiring.

Cypresses should be cut back only at points where wood has already formed. New shoots should be pinched back by hand. With this method, the scale closest to the trunk usually remains undamaged and does not turn brown as it would if cut back. New shoots on younger specimens should be allowed to grow longer than those on older trees. The more frequently new growth is pinched back, the denser the foliage will become. However, pinching it back less frequently and allowing the tree to grow more freely will encourage the branches to grow thicker.
Acquiring a plant: Monterey cypresses of various ages and sizes can be bought as pot plants. They can also be purchased sometimes in specialist bonsai shops. However, such specimens have usually not been trained to any great extent, but merely kept small.
Pests: Monterey cypresses are susceptible to attack by spider mites, mealy bugs and scale insects.

Pinching back a new shoot

Cupressus macrocarpa *'Goldcrest', young plant*

Elaeagnus
Elaeagnus or oleaster   ○

The *Elaeagnus* genus includes evergreen and deciduous woody plants that usually grow as shrubs, although they sometimes also develop into small trees. Most species come from Asia. The tough-textured, usually oval leaves, dark green on top and lighter on the underside, are arranged alternately on the branches. In some varieties, the simple flowers develop into fruits that resemble gooseberries, not all of which are edible. To develop satisfactorily, plants in the elaeagnus family must be kept outdoors for at least part of the year.

Position: light and sunny all year round. An elaeagnus should spend the summer on a balcony or in the garden. In winter, place it in a cool, unheated room. It will tolerate temperatures almost down to but not lower than 0°C (32°F).

Soil: a mix of two parts fired clay particles, one part sand and one part potting compost. Two-thirds should be replaced every two to three years, and the roots should be pruned at the same time.

Watering: keep very moist in summer. And even in winter, all species in this family need relatively frequent watering because of their large leaves. If they are allowed to dry out, they will lose a lot of foliage. Normal tap water can be used.

Feeding: every two weeks from early spring to autumn with an organic or inorganic fertilizer. A monthly feed is sufficient in winter.

Training: because the leaves are relatively large, a minimum height of 40cm (16in) should be aimed for. All the Japanese styles are feasible. One- or two-year-old branches can be easily trained with wire; older limbs will have to be guyed down. Plants in the elaeagnus family produce shoots that gain in length very quickly and initially have only leaf buds. Leaves do not emerge until later, and on young plants they should be allowed to grow to a certain size before pruning begins. Wait until the new shoot has reached a length of between 15 and 20cm (6 and 8in) before cutting it back as far as necessary for the shape of crown you wish to achieve, usually to between one and three leaves. Older, well-developed plants that have already been trained can be pruned at an earlier stage. This will encourage denser twiggy growth.

Acquiring a plant: elaeagnus can be propagated from cuttings, and some species are sold in nurseries as garden plants. These are less suited for cultivation as bonsais. Young bonsais, and sometimes older, well-trained specimens, can be bought in specialist bonsai shops.

Pests: elaeagnus is fairly susceptible to mealy bug and scale insect infestation.

Elaeagnus, *about twenty years old*

Ficus benjamina
Weeping fig ○ – ◑

The weeping fig is a tropical plant. It has a short trunk with smooth, silvery-grey bark and outstretched branches supported by numerous aerial roots. A large number of different varieties are available as houseplants, including some with very small leaves.

Since this plant is already familiar to many people as a houseplant and is relatively easy to keep, it is a good choice for cultivation as a bonsai.

Position: can be kept indoors all year round in a warm, bright to partially shaded spot. It tolerates temperatures between 12 and 28°C (53 and 82°F) and can be kept near a radiator. It can also be moved outdoors in summer, either to a balcony or into the garden. However, it should be allowed to adjust to direct sunlight very gradually.

Soil: a mix of equal parts of fired clay particles, sand and potting compost. Other mixtures can also be used successfully. The soil should be changed once a year. Older plants need be repotted only once every two years.

Watering: use tap water that has been left to stand and water as soon as the soil surface feels dry or only slightly moist.

Feeding: from spring to autumn, with plenty of organic or inorganic fertilizer. Halve the dose in winter.

Training: weeping figs can be successfully grown in all the Japanese styles. Because of the relatively large leaves, any bonsai should be designed with a final height of at least 50cm (20in) in mind. Since a wide range of untrained pot plants of various ages is readily available in florists shops and garden centres, this species is particularly suitable for those making their first attempt at cultivating a bonsai. New shoots should be trimmed back to one to three leaves once they have reached a length of about 20cm (8in). In the top third of the crown, new shoots should always be kept short to encourage the development of the lower branches. It is often necessary to cut back into old wood to keep the tree compact. The plant is quick to put out new shoots after being pruned in this way.

The branches remain flexible for a long time, which makes them easy to shape with wire. The branches thicken very quickly, so a constant eye should be kept on the wire; it often needs to be removed after six to eight weeks to stop it becoming ingrown. Damage caused by excessively tight wire remains visible for a long time.

Acquiring a plant: cuttings are easy to establish in a rooting medium. A wide range of young plants and untrained pot plants can be bought in ordinary florists shops and in garden centres. Bonsais of variable quality can be bought in specialist shops. Small-leaved varieties are also suitable for cultivation as miniature bonsais.

Pests: the weeping fig is susceptible to scale insect infestation. Spider mite infestation causes yellow speckling on the leaves, but does not lead to loss of foliage until later. Weeping figs can often survive satisfactorily with a certain level of mite infestation. However, their rate of development will be slowed down considerably.

Ficus benjamina, *about thirty years old, Rüger collection*

Ficus buxifolia
Box-leaf fig ○ – ◑

This species of fig, a native of Africa, has noticeably small, dark-green, smooth-edged leaves, blunt at the tip and similar to those of the boxes. The trunk and branches of this evergreen tree have dark-brown bark. The flowers develop singly from the leaf axils, sometimes in great profusion, and give way to small, inedible fruits that start off green and then turn reddish-brown.

Its small leaves make F. buxifolia well suited to cultivation as a small bonsai.

Position: light, but shaded from the hot midday sun. The plant can be moved outdoors in summer, on to a balcony or into the garden, provided it is allowed to acclimatize gradually to its new location. It needs to be kept in a warm spot in winter. If it is placed close to a radiator or other heat source, it is a good idea to stand it on a shallow tray filled with water and hygroscopic pellets to raise the humidity level in the immediate vicinity of the plant.
Soil: a mix of equal parts of fired clay particles, sand and potting compost. Other soil mixes are also possible.
Watering: the plant should not be kept too moist. Do not water until the soil surface is slightly dry. If it is given too much or too little water, the plant will shed its foliage. Normal tap water can be used.
Feeding: every two weeks in the growing season with an organic or inorganic fertilizer. From late autumn to early spring, feed just once a month.
Training: the branches do not retain their flexibility for as long as those of other species of fig. For this reason, the measures required to create a bonsai should be carried out at short, fairly regular intervals. All the Japanese styles are feasible, and F. buxifolia is also easy to cultivate as a miniature bonsai.

One- to two-year-old branches can be wired, but older ones will have to be guyed down. The wire must be inspected regularly and removed if it is getting too tight.

Once they have reached a length of 5–10cm (2–4in), new shoots should be trimmed back to between one and five leaves, depending on the desired final height.
Acquiring a plant: F. buxifolia can be propagated from cuttings. Young plants can sometimes be purchased in ordinary florists or specialist shops. The plants sold as bonsais are usually only a few years old. Older specimens are very seldom offered for sale.
Pests: rare cases of scale insect infestation.

Ficus carica
Common fig ○

This deciduous species, particularly widely cultivated in Mediterranean regions, develops into large bushes or trees. Older specimens have strikingly long branches, whose own weight forces them to droop to the ground.
Even in older trees, the trunk remains smooth. Young branches can be remarkably thick. The large, three-lobed leaves emerge in spring and are arranged alternately. The inconspicuous flowers develop into edible fruits.

Its large leaves make the common fig suitable for cultivation as a bonsai only under certain circumstances. As the number of branches increases, the leaves become smaller and smaller, so that a thoroughly attractive bonsai can be

Ficus buxifolia, *young plant*

Ficus carica, *about eight years old*

needed, and the soil surface should be allowed to dry out slightly between waterings. Tap water is quite suitable.

Feeding: young plants should be fed weekly from early spring to autumn with an inorganic liquid fertilizer; older, more mature plants, whose leaves are to remain small, should be fed about once a month.

Training: training a common fig is not easy because of its thick branches and large leaves. However, all styles of bonsai are feasible.

In spring, before the new leaves emerge, all the previous year's growth should be severely cut back. New branches will not develop unless at least the tips of the shoots are removed. Any cuts must be well sealed to prevent the remaining buds from drying out and to avoid infections. Older branches can be removed at any time during the year.

One-year-old branches are easily trained by wiring. Older branches become inflexible and so have to be guyed down to avoid damaging the bark.

Acquiring a plant: seeds can be obtained from the fruits, which should be soaked in water for a few days so that the flesh comes away easily. The seeds can then be sown straight away. Young specimens can sometimes be bought as pot plants. Common figs are seldom sold in specialist bonsai shops.

Pests: the common fig is sometimes attacked by scale insects.

produced if the tree is allowed to grow to a reasonable height.

Position: In summer, common figs will be happy in a sunny spot out of doors. In winter, they are best kept in a cool room indoors. As soon as new shoots emerge, they can be moved onto a balcony or patio.

Soil: a mix of two parts fired clay particles, one part sand and one part potting compost. Other soil mixes are also possible.

Watering: the soil can be kept constantly moist in summer. In winter, when the leaves have dropped, less water is

Ficus microcarpa
Laurel fig ○

In its natural habitat, this evergreen species grows into a tree with tough-textured, alternate leaves. Berry-shaped fruits develop from the leaf axils; they are initially green and then turn yellow or purplish. They are not edible.
The laurel fig is hardy and ideally suited for cultivation as a houseplant, which makes it a good choice for newcomers to the art of bonsai.

Ficus microcarpa

Position: bright and sunny, but protected from direct midday sun. In summer, the plant can be moved out of doors on to a balcony or into the garden. In winter, the laurel fig will flourish in a warm room where the temperature is between 19 and 24°C (66 and 75°F). It can even be placed next to a radiator.
Soil: a mix of equal parts of fired clay particles, sand and potting compost. Since laurel figs are usually sold in a different soil mix, they should be accustomed gradually to the new, more loamy soil. Half the soil must be changed at least every two years.
Watering: a laurel fig should be kept evenly moist. If it is too wet or too dry, it will shed its foliage. However, it prefers being dry to being waterlogged. Normal tap water is quite suitable.
Feeding: every two weeks from spring to autumn with an organic or inorganic fertilizer. For the rest of the year, feed just once a month.
Training: because the branches thicken quickly and retain their flexibility for several years, the laurel fig makes good bonsai material. To produce a powerful trunk, young plants should have their trunks cut back severely several times.

Since most of the leaves will be removed at the same time, the plant's demand for water will fall drastically. The soil surface should be allowed to dry out between waterings.

The trunk and branches can be shaped with wire. To produce powerful limbs, new shoots should be cut back to one to five leaves once they have reached a length of about 20cm (8in). If the plant already has sturdy branches and twiggy growth is to be encouraged, the tip of each new shoot can be removed once a length of 5cm (2in) has been reached. This will encourage the growth of buds further down the shoot.
Acquiring a plant: the laurel fig can be propagated from cuttings. Young plants are sometimes sold in specialist shops. Trees already cultivated as bonsais can be bought in various shapes and styles.
Pests: laurel figs cultivated as bonsais are hardly ever attacked by pests.

Ficus natalensis
Natal fig ○

This variety of fig, a native of Africa, has branches with narrow, elongated, densely packed leaves, tough, blunt, and dark green in colour.

This evergreen plant can grow into large shrubs or imposing trees. The Natal fig is one of the hardiest of fig species and is therefore particularly recommended for beginners.

Position: warm and bright; direct sunlight can be tolerated from time to time. In summer, the Natal fig can be moved out of doors, onto a balcony or into the garden. It must be allowed to acclimatize gradually to direct sunlight. From early autumn, the tree should be brought indoors and placed in a warm room where the temperature is between 18 and 24°C (64 and 75°F).
Soil: a mix of equal parts of fired clay particles, sand and potting compost. If a different mix is used, it should be well draining. Half the soil should be changed every two years.
Watering: keep reasonably moist. Normal tap water is quite suitable.
Feeding: every two weeks from early spring to autumn with an organic or inorganic fertilizer. During colder periods of the year, monthly feeds are sufficient.
Training: the Natal fig can be easily trimmed into the broom style. For any other style, you will probably have to resort to wiring. One- to three-year-old branches that have not grown too thick can be shaped with wire. Thick or older, less flexible branches will have to be guyed down to a wire threaded through the bottom of the container.

On young developing plants that have still to grow a lot thicker, new shoots should be cut back to 1–5cm (0.4–2in), depending on their position in the crown, once they have reached a length of 15–20cm (6–8in). Older, more mature bonsais should be cut back at an earlier stage.
Acquiring a plant: the Natal fig can be easily propagated from cuttings. Young plants can occasionally be bought in specialist shops, as can young specimens already trained as bonsais.
Pests: the Natal fig is not very susceptible to pest infestation.

Ficus natalensis, *about ten years old,* Rüger collection

Ficus religiosa
Bo tree or sacred fig tree ◑ – ○

This evergreen tree, a native of India and Sri Lanka, has powerful, greyish branches that bear alternate, heart-shaped, smooth-edged leaves, 8–12cm (3–5in) in length, with prominent veins. The quiver-like flowers give way to inedible fruits that turn purple when ripe. To Buddhists and Hindus, *F. religiosa* is a sacred tree. The large leaves make it essential to aim for a minimum height of 50cm (20in).

Position: the bo tree likes a bright or sunny location. If there is not enough light, it quickly sheds its foliage. It is quite happy out of doors in the summer, although it should be accustomed gradually to direct sun and strong wind. In winter, it is best kept in a warm room in which the humidity is no lower than 40%.

Soil: a mix of equal parts of fired clay particles, sand and potting compost. Other soil mixes are also possible. If it is watered solely with tap water, one-third of the soil should be changed each year.

Watering: the plant must be kept evenly moist. However, it is more tolerant of dryness than of excessive watering. If it is constantly waterlogged, it will lose its leaves. Tap water is suitable.

Feeding: every two weeks from early spring to mid-autumn, and once a month in winter. Either organic or inorganic fertilizers can be used.

Training: *F. religiosa* is not suitable for creating small bonsais. Otherwise, all styles are feasible.

One- and two-year-old branches can be shaped with wire. The wire should be checked regularly. In the warmer months, the wire may well become too tight after just a few weeks. If this is the case, it should be removed and replaced if necessary. Older branches should be guyed down, in order to avoid damage to the bark.

In young plants, and depending on the position in the crown, new shoots should be cut back to between one and five leaves once they have reached a length of 10–20cm (4–8in). Older plants can be pruned earlier. *F. religiosa* does not develop new branches as readily as other *Ficus* species.

Acquiring a plant: the bo tree can be propagated from cuttings. Young plants are not available commercially. Very occasionally, you might see already trained specimens in specialist bonsai shops.

Pests: *F. religiosa* sometimes falls prey to spider mites.

Ficus salicifolia
Willow-leaved fig ○ – ◑

This evergreen fig, which can reach enormous heights in its natural habitat, has lanceolate leaves arranged alternately and at short distances along its branches. Even young plants bear flowers from which berry-shaped fruits develop, initially green in colour, later turning reddish or purplish-brown.

This tree can be very easily trimmed into an imposing broom style. Although it often loses all its foliage if its care is disrupted in any way or if there are any other changes in the external environment, it can also be grown by beginners.

Position: light, by a window, but protected from the midday sun. It can be moved outdoors in summer. When it is brought back inside, it usually sheds all

Ficus religiosa, *about twenty years old,*
after leaf pruning

Ficus salicifolia, *about eight years old*

its leaves. If placed in a warm room
where the humidity level is not too low,
F. *religiosa* will soon produce new
shoots.
Soil: a mix of equal parts of fired clay
particles, sand and potting compost.
Other well-draining soil mixes can also
be used. If only tap water is used, half
the soil should be changed once a year.

Watering: keep evenly moist. Once the
fig has lost all its leaves, do not water
again until the soil surface has dried
out a little. Ordinary tap water is
quite suitable.
Feeding: every two weeks from spring to
mid-autumn, otherwise just once a
month. Use an organic or inorganic
fertilizer.
Training: this fig can be easily trimmed
into the broom style; wiring is not
usually necessary. However, other styles
are also possible.

Two-year-old branches that have
already lost their leaves can usually be
wired, but because of the dense foliage it
is difficult to shape younger branches
with wire without losing leaves.
Branches more than three years old have
to be guyed down to protect the bark.

Depending on the branch's position in
the crown and the length it is ultimately
to attain, new shoots can be cut back to
1–5cm (0.4–2in) once they have reached
a length of 10–20cm (4–8in). Older
bonsais can be pruned at an earlier stage.
Acquiring a plant: this plant can be easily
propagated from cuttings. Young
specimens can sometimes be purchased in
specialist bonsai shops, as can trees that
have already been trained.
Pests: F. *salicifolia* is very susceptible to
spider mite infestation, which causes it to
shed all its leaves. Without treatment, the plant will not put out any
more shoots.

71

Fuchsia
Fuchsia ◑

Fuchsias are subtropical plants from South and Central America. They are familiar mainly as plants for window boxes or hanging baskets, although in their natural habitat they often develop into fairly large shrubs. The leaves of this deciduous genus vary in shape and size from species to species, although they are often lanceolate and always arranged in opposite pairs or whorls. The distinctive flowers appear in large numbers in summer, developing from the axils of the terminal leaves.

For anyone with experience of cultivating fuchsias as pot plants, a fuchsia bonsai can be a wonderful addition to a collection.

Fuchsia, *about ten years old, Stirnberg collection*

Position: in summer, the best spot for a fuchsia is a light but shaded location, either indoors or outdoors. Once the first frosts can be expected, it should be moved to a cold, frost-free, shaded spot, even if it is already indoors. Most fuchsias are sensitive to frost, so they should not be moved outdoors too early in spring.

Soil: a mix of equal parts of fired clay particles, sand, and peat. Other soil mixes can also be used.

Watering: water generously in summer, more sparingly in winter. Normal tap water is quite satisfactory.

Feeding: every two weeks from the first new shoots to early autumn. An organic fertilizer is suitable. Virtually no feeding is required in winter.

Training: training should begin at a very early stage, since even one-year-old branches are very inflexible. The direction of growth is therefore established very early. However, young branches can be wired with care. Depending on the final size to be achieved and the thickness of branch required, new shoots can be cut back to one to three pairs of leaves once they have reached a length of 5–20cm (2–8 in).

Acquiring a plant: fuchsias are easy to propagate by cuttings. Time can be saved by taking a pot plant as your starting material. Specialist bonsai shops seldom have fuchsias for sale.

Pests: Fuchsias are frequently attacked by whitefly, and greenfly infestation is also fairly common.

Haematoxylum campechianum, *about forty years old, Rüger collection*

Haematoxylum campechianum
Bloodwood tree ○

This evergreen tree, a native of Central and South America, has prickly branches bearing paripinnate leaves that close up as the light fades at nightfall. Cuts exude a red sap. The yellowish flowers form small, spherical inflorescences.

   H. campechianum is very seldom sold as a bonsai. It needs a very warm, sunny environment, with high humidity. It is not suitable for beginners.

Position: bright, sunny, and warm all year round. The plant can be moved to a sunny spot out of doors for the summer months, although it needs to be accustomed gradually to its new location. In winter, it should be placed in a room where the temperature is higher than 20°C (68°F). To increase the humidity level, place the plant on a shallow tray filled with water and hygroscopic pellets. The soil should not be in direct contact with the water in the tray.

Soil: a mix of equal parts of fired clay particles, sand and potting compost. With young plants, a third of the soil should be changed every year; with older bonsais, this need be done only once every three years.

Watering: keep the plant evenly moist. In winter, the water should not be too cold. Do not use hard tap water.

Feeding: every two weeks from spring to late summer, and once a month in the colder seasons. Use an organic fertilizer.

Training: if training starts early enough, all the established styles are feasible. One- and two-year-old branches can be shaped with wire. Older limbs should be guyed down, to prevent damage to the bark.

   With young plants, new shoots should be cut back to one to three leaves once they have reached a length of 15cm (6in). With older plants, pruning can begin earlier.

Acquiring a plant: *H. campechianum* can be propagated from cuttings. Young plants are not usually sold in the normal retail outlets, although you may occasionally come across older and therefore more expensive specimens.

Pests: *H. campechianum* is seldom attacked by pests.

Hibiscus rosa-sinensis
Rose of China ○

This evergreen shrub is found throughout the tropics, and probably came originally from China. In unfavourable conditions, it will shed all its long, ovate, opposite leaves. There are numerous varieties, with flowers of different colours and shapes, many of which can be bought as pot plants. Because of its relatively large leaves, the rose of China is seldom cultivated as a bonsai. Nevertheless, if the plant is allowed to reach a minimum height of 40cm (16cm), then the proportions may be perfectly acceptable.

Position: bright and sunny all year round. In summer, the plant can be moved out of doors. However, the move usually causes it to shed a lot of foliage, although it will quickly grow back again. A hibiscus bonsai should be brought back indoors in winter and placed in a room where the temperature is between 16 and 20°C (61 and 68°F).
Soil: a mix of equal parts of fired clay particles, sand and peat. Young plants need to have their soil changed once a year, older ones less often. When the plant is repotted, the roots should be pruned at the same time.
Watering: *H. rosa-sinensis* needs a lot of water in both summer and winter. The plant should also be watered regularly, because irregular watering causes the flowers to drop. Tap water is perfectly suitable.
Feeding: every two weeks from mid-spring to early autumn with an organic fertilizer. For the rest of the year, monthly feeds are adequate.
Training: A hibiscus is not easy to train, since its branches quickly become inflexible and very thick. Nor does it form new branches readily.

Young shoots can be shaped as desired through the careful use of wire. Older branches should be guyed down. New shoots should be cut back to one to three leaves once they have reached a length of 10–20cm (4–8in).

To establish the basic shape as soon as possible, young plants should be encouraged not to bloom in the first few years. With older plants, shorter shoots can be cut back once the flowering season is over.
Acquiring a plant: Hibiscus can be propagated from cuttings. To save time, however, it is best to use a pot plant, which may be two or three years old. As already noted above, florists and garden centres usually stock a wide range of varieties. Hibiscus bonsais are not available commercially.
Pests: whitefly infestation is common. In severe cases, expert advice should be sought.

Lagerstroemia indica
Crape myrtle ○

This deciduous shrub, a native of China and Korea but now widely used as an ornamental plant in all tropical countries, has a smooth, light-brown trunk. The opposite, oval leaves are reddish at first, turning green later. The flowers appear in summer, when the days are longest. There are many varieties with flowers of different colours and shapes.

The crape myrtle is one of the few deciduous shrubs that can be kept as a houseplant. However, it requires a good deal of warmth and sunlight in the summer if its flowers are to develop in all their splendour.

Hibiscus rosa-sinensis, *about eight years old*

Lagerstroemia indica, *about ten years old*

Position: bright and sunny during the growing season. During spring and summer, the crape myrtle can also be kept out of doors. It will flower only if it receives plenty of sunlight. Sometimes it fails to flower altogether. In winter, it should be placed in a frost-free location but does not require quite so much light. The darker the winter location is, the colder it should be.

Soil: a mix of equal parts of fired clay particles, sand and potting compost.

Other well-draining soil mixes have also been used successfully.

Watering: when it is bearing leaves, the plant can be kept very moist. If the root-ball is allowed to dry out, new shoots will die off. In winter, it requires only a little water. Rainwater or water with a low mineral salt content should be used.

Feeding: every two weeks as soon as the first leaves appear in spring. From autumn to spring, there is no need to feed the plant at all.

Training: if training begins at an early stage, then all styles are feasible. One- and two-year-old branches can be shaped with wire. Older branches tend to be hard and brittle and therefore more difficult to train. The best way to shape such limbs is by hard pruning. With young plants that need to develop powerful branches, new shoots should not be pruned until after the leaves have dropped. On the other hand, if you want to promote twiggy growth on branches that have already grown sufficiently thick, then new shoots should be cut back to between one and three pairs of leaves once they have reached a length of 10cm (4 in). If pruning takes place during the growing season, few flowers will be produced, since most of the flower buds will be lost.

Acquiring a plant: crape myrtle can be propagated from cuttings. It is sometimes available as a pot plant in florists shops.

Unfortunately, trained specimens seldom find their way into specialist bonsai shops. For this reason, it is rare to find it cultivated as a bonsai.

Pests: the crape myrtle is very susceptible to greenfly infestation.

Lantana camara
Yellow sage   ○

This evergreen shrub, a native of South America, is widespread throughout the tropics. The leaves are arranged alternately on the square branches. The flowers emerge in summer in dense clusters that develop from the leaf axils. The colour of the flowers changes in the course of the flowering season. The black berries are poisonous!

Many forms and cultivars are grown. Because the branches tend to be spindly and the leaves are sometimes widely spaced, *L. camara* is quite difficult to train. However, the splendidly showy flowers make it worth a try.

Position: bright and sunny. The plant should be placed outdoors in summer. In winter, it will be happy in an unheated room.
Soil: a mix of equal parts of fired clay particles, sand and peat. Other soil mixes are also possible.
Watering: *L. camara* needs a lot of water in summer and should never be allowed to dry out. In its cool winter location, it needs less water. *L. camara* is as sensitive to dryness as it is to being waterlogged. Ordinary tap water is quite suitable.
Feeding: every two weeks from spring until autumn with an organic or inorganic fertilizer. Monthly feeds are sufficient in winter.
Training: all styles are feasible. Because of the long-stalked flower clusters, the shape being aimed for is often discernible only in winter and spring. During the flowering season, the structure of the bonsai is often obscured to a large extent. The spindly branches make it

necessary to aim for a minimum height of 40cm (16in). In autumn and once in spring, *L. camara* should be pruned hard, right back to the largest limbs. Once the new year's growth has reached a length of 20cm (8in), young plants should be cut back to one or two leaf pairs, with no attempt being made to spare flower buds. This should be repeated as necessary until autumn. Older, well-established plants can be pinched back from May onwards (see p. 60). This will encourage twiggy growth and ensure that the flowers do not develop too far beyond the actual crown area.

Only young branches can be wired. Older branches that have not yet grown too thick can sometimes be styled by using suspended wiring.
Acquiring a plant: *L. camara* can be propagated from cuttings. It is usually planted in flower beds or in window boxes. Consequently, a wide range of different varieties is available each spring in garden centres as pot plants. Trained specimens are sometimes sold in specialist bonsai shops, but the styling is not usually very far advanced.
Pests: *L. camara* is regularly attacked by greenfly, spider mite, and whitefly.

Lantana camara, *about ten years old*

Leptospermum scoparium ○ – ◑
Manuka or New Zealand tea tree

The evergreen manuka is a native of Australia, New Zealand, and Malaysia, where it grows mostly as a shrub, and sometimes as a small tree. The small, lanceolate, bluish-green leaves are arranged alternately. The single flowers appear in summer and are remarkably close set; they vary in colour from white to dark red and develop a hard, cylindrical seed capsule. After a few years, the bark on the branches and the trunk bursts open to form feathery shreds, giving even fairly young plants the appearance of great age.

Because of the particular demands the manuka makes of its position, only experienced bonsai enthusiasts will have any chance of keeping one for any length of time.

Position: bright and cool all year round. It can be moved out of doors in summer. Its winter location must be frost-free, with a high humidity level.

Soil: *L. scoparium* needs an acidic soil. So you should use either peat or the azalea granules that can be bought in bonsai shops. It reacts very sensitively to hard root pruning, so only 20% of the soil should be changed each year, with the roots being cut back at the same time.

Watering: always keep very moist. Rainwater is to be preferred. If the root-ball dries out, the plant will die. *L. scoparium* is more tolerant of excessive than of insufficient watering.

Feeding: with organic or even peat-based fertilizers; the latter should be used with caution, however.

Training: the manuka can be trimmed into all styles. Its very small leaves make it very suitable for cultivation as a miniature bonsai.

One- and two-year-old branches can be easily wired. Older branches become brittle and fragile, but suspended wiring can be used with care. However, they are liable to break off at the trunk. As the limb is bent into shape, the breaking point should be protected with the thumb.

With small bonsais, new growth should be cut back once the shoots have reached a length of about 10cm (4in), although with larger trees pruning should be left until later. The flowers emerge in summer, and sometimes for a second time in winter. From late spring until the flowering season, pruning can stop if a good array of blossoms is desired.

Acquiring a plant: the manuka can be propagated from cuttings. It is also sold as a pot plant; such specimens are usually several years old. Small manuka bonsais can also be bought in specialist bonsai shops.

Pests: *L. scoparium* is seldom attacked by pests.

Flowers of L. scoparium

Leptospermum scoparium, *young plant*

Ligustrum japonicum
Japanese privet ○ – ◑

This evergreen shrub, a native of Japan and Korea, has smooth branches that bear alternate, broad, egg-shaped leaves. The white flowers, from which poisonous black berries develop, are borne in large panicles.

If an unheated room is available as a winter location, then a Japanese privet can be grown by a beginner.

Position: bright, partially shaded or sunny if out of doors. From spring to autumn, the Japanese privet can be placed outside, either on a balcony or in the garden. However, it must be protected from frost. It can be moved to an unheated room in winter.
Soil: a mix of equal parts of fired clay particles, sand and potting compost. Two-thirds of the soil should be changed every two years.
Watering: keep evenly moist. The plant tolerates temporary dryness. Ordinary tap water is quite suitable.
Feeding: every two weeks during the growing period with an organic fertilizer. In winter, the interval between feeds can be stretched to between four and six weeks.
Training: if training begins early enough, all styles are feasible. The upright and broom styles are particularly popular. One- and two-year-old branches can be easily wired. To avoid visible scars on the bark, older limbs should be guyed down.

Depending on the plant's stage of development, new growth can be cut back to between one and five leaf pairs once the shoot has attained a length of 5–20cm (2–8in).

Ligustrum japonicum, *about six years old*

Acquiring a plant: L. *japonicum* can be easily propagated from cuttings and can also be bought as a bonsai.
Pests: L. *japonicum* is seldom attacked by pests.

Malpighia coccigera
Miniature holly ○ – ◑

This evergreen shrub, which has its origins in the West Indies, has small, tough-textured leaves that are glossy on top, spiny-toothed on the edges and arranged alternately. In summer, pinkish flowers appear in profusion, from which small red berries develop.

Only experienced bonsai enthusiasts will be able to keep a miniature holly for any length of time. Beginners should not be tempted to buy one, however attractive it may appear.

Position: indoors, in a well-lit spot by a window. It must be shaded from direct midday sun, however. In summer, the plant can be moved to a similar position out of doors, i.e. shaded from direct sun but nevertheless with plenty of light. In winter, it requires a minimum temperature no lower than 20°C (68°F). The humidity level must not fall below 50%. Good results can be achieved if the plant can be placed on a heating pad during the winter. The soil temperature should not fall below 22°C (72°F).
Soil: a mix of one part fired clay particles, one part sand and two parts potting compost. It is important that the soil should be well draining. One-third of the soil should be changed every two years; at the same time, the roots should be pruned carefully.
Watering: the soil must be kept evenly moist. It will respond to under- and over-watering by shedding its leaves. Use rainwater, making sure that it is not too cold in winter (room temperature).
Feeding: every three weeks from spring to late autumn with an organic fertilizer. Feed every four to six weeks in winter.
Training: all the classic styles are feasible. The broom style can be achieved only with careful selective pruning. If you want to aim for another style, branches must be shaped with wire at an early stage. One- and two-year-old branches can still be shaped to some extent. Older limbs become very inflexible and have to be guyed down.

Depending on the size of the tree and the branch's position in the crown, new growth should be cut back to between one and three leaf pairs as soon the shoot has reached a length of 10–15cm.
Acquiring a plant: *M. coccigera* can be propagated from cuttings, which should be planted in soil that has been warmed. Older cuttings can sometimes be bought as pot plants. The plant is often available only as a bonsai.
Pests: *M. coccigera* is not very susceptible to pest attack.

Malpighia coccigera, *young plant*

Metrosideros excelsa
New Zealand Christmas tree ○

This evergreen plant, a native of New Zealand, grows as a large shrub or small tree in the wild. The lanceolate to ovate leaves are arranged in opposite pairs. It flowers in early spring.

Because of its relatively small leaves, the New Zealand Christmas tree is suited to cultivation as a miniature bonsai.

Position: a bright spot, with several hours of direct sunlight. The plant can be kept out of doors in summer. In winter, it is best kept in an unheated room.

Soil: a mix of equal parts of Japanese azalea granules, fired clay particles, sand and potting compost. If tap water is used, one-third of the soil must be changed each year, with the roots being pruned at the same time.

Watering: rainwater is to be preferred. If it is not available, tap water that has been left to stand or boiled can be used. In summer, the plant should be kept very moist. In winter, do not water until the soil surface has dried out.

Feeding: with organic fertilizer. The plant should be fed every two weeks from spring to late summer, and once a month in winter.

Training: all styles are feasible. If you wish to avoid the use of wire, the plant can be easily trimmed into the broom style. Other styles will require the use of wire or suspended wiring.

Two-year-old branches can be shaped as desired with the use of wire. Older branches will have to be guyed down to avoid leaving permanent pressure marks on the bark. Small bonsais should be cut back to one or two leaf pairs once new

Metrosideros excelsa, *about ten years old, Prinsler and Werner collection*

Murraya paniculata, *about twenty years old, Rüger collection*

growth has reached a length of 5–10cm (2–4in). Larger specimens can be allowed to grow a little longer. This will encourage the trunk to grow thicker.

Acquiring a plant: the New Zealand Christmas tree can be propagated from cuttings. It is increasingly being sold as a ready-styled bonsai.

Pests: there are no known pests that particularly favour the New Zealand Christmas tree.

Murraya paniculata
Orange jasmine   ○ – ◑

This evergreen tree or large shrub, a native of Asia, has a pale, smooth bark, pinnate foliage, and highly fragrant, white flowers borne in clusters. Only a few flowers in any one cluster open at the same time. Once these have faded, the others open out. Pollinated flowers give rise to small, ovoid, inedible fruits, orange to bright red in colour.

The orange jasmine is suitable for beginners to the art of bonsai. However, its well-branched, rather unkempt appearance means it is not particularly popular.

Position: a light, partially shaded spot indoors all year round. In summer, it can also be moved outdoors to a place shaded from the midday sun. In the colder months, however, it should be placed in a heated room where the temperature is around 20°C (68°F). The humidity level should not be too low.

Soil: a mix of two parts fired clay particles, one part sand and one part potting compost. Half the soil must be changed at least every two years.

Watering: in the first few weeks after repotting, the plant should not be immersed in water since it would remain wet for too long. Water when the soil surface is still just slightly moist. Tap water is perfectly suitable. However, if the plant is kept indoors all year round, so that it never receives any rainwater, the soil should be completely renewed once a year.

Feeding: young plants should be fed at least every two weeks with an organic or

inorganic fertilizer. Older specimens can be fed once a month until the flowers appear, and then more frequently.

Training: the pinnate foliage, which tends to grow unmanageably in all directions, makes the orange jasmine unsuitable for cultivation as a miniature bonsai. A minimum height of 50cm (20in) should be aimed for, otherwise the foliage may obscure the outline of the shape you are seeking to achieve. All styles are feasible.

One- and two-year-old branches can be wired. Older branches can sometimes be persuaded to change their direction if guyed down to a wire threaded through the bottom of the container.

Young plants should be trimmed back to between one and three leaves once new shoots have reached a length of 20cm (8in). Older, sturdier specimens can be trimmed to one or two leaves once the new growth is 10cm (4in) in length.

Acquiring a plant: the orange jasmine is often sold in bonsai shops, although the specimens you will come across here vary widely in age and the extent to which they have been styled. Cuttings will put down roots easily, and some shops now sell cuttings that have already taken root.

Pests: the orange jasmine is susceptible mainly to scale insect infestation. In a dry atmosphere, it can also fall prey to spider mites.

Myrciaria cauliflora
Jaboticaba ○ – ◑

This fruiting, evergreen tree, a native of Central and South America, has a short trunk, the bark of which flakes off in large patches to give a mottled appearance reminiscent of a plane tree. The trunk is well branched, and the very irregular, light-brown limbs bear opposite, ovoid to lanceolate leaves, smooth edged, and light green in colour.

The white flowers, borne in clusters directly on the trunk and branches, develop later into edible, grape-like fruits. Its irregular growth pattern and small leaves make this a popular plant for cultivation as an indoor bonsai.

Position: a light, partially shaded spot. The plant can be moved outdoors in summer. In winter, it can be placed in an unheated room, provided the humidity level does not drop below 50%. If that is not possible, put it in an unheated room where the temperature is unlikely to fall below 12°C (53°F).
Soil: a mix of two parts fired clay particles, one part sand and two parts potting compost. Young plants should have their soil changed once a year; older specimens can remain in the same soil for two years.
Watering: use water with a low mineral salt content. If you have no rainwater, distilled water can be used, mixed with an equal volume of tap water. The plant should be watered when the soil surface is still just slightly moist.
Feeding: every two to three weeks during the growing season with an organic fertilizer. Feed once a month in winter.
Training: of all the Japanese styles, the plant's natural habit is closest to the broom style. However, other styles are also feasible.

One- to three-year-old branches can be shaped by wiring. Older, sturdier limbs will have to be guyed down.

New shoots do not grow very long without changing their direction of growth. Very often, new shoots stop growing once they are 10cm (4in) or so in length. They have a brief rest before branching out again from the tip and starting to grow in two different directions.

The best time for pruning is during the brief resting period, before the new twigs start to grow. To keep the shape compact, the tree can be cut back to old wood, from which new shoots will readily sprout.
Acquiring a plant: M. cauliflora can be bought in specialist bonsai shops in various stages of development. It can also be propagated from cuttings.
Pests: the tree is susceptible to greenfly infestation.

Myrsine africana
Myrsine ○

This small evergreen shrub, found in both Africa and Asia, carries small, firm, round, opposite leaves. The size of its leaves makes it particularly suitable for cultivation as a miniature bonsai.

Position: a bright spot all year round. The plant can also spend the summer out of doors. In winter, it should be placed in a cool, unheated room.
Soil: a mix of equal parts of fired clay particles, sand and potting compost. Half the soil can be changed each year.
Watering: keep very moist in summer. Water less frequently in winter. Ordinary tap water is quite suitable.

Myrciaria cauliflora, *about fifteen years old*, Prinsler and Werner collection

Myrsine africana, *about ten years old*, Prinsler and Werner collection

Feeding: once the new growth emerges in spring, feed the plant every two weeks with an organic fertilizer. From early autumn onwards, monthly feeds are sufficient.

Training: all styles are feasible, but the broom style is very popular. The plant can be trimmed into this style without resorting to wire.

The dense crown makes the branches difficult to wire without removing some of the secondary branches at the same time. One- to three-year-old branches are still flexible enough to be styled. A wire put in place in spring can often be left for a whole year, since the limbs do not thicken very quickly.

Once new growth is 5cm (2in) in length, it should be trimmed back to between one and three leaf pairs. If an entirely new branch is to be developed, do not prune until the new shoot has reached a length of 20cm (8in).

Acquiring a plant: *M. africana* can be easily propagated from cuttings. It can also be bought as a bonsai in various stages of training.

Pests: there are no known pests with a particular predilection for *M. africana*.

Myrtus communis
Common myrtle　　　　○ – ◑

This evergreen shrub, found in Mediterranean regions and west Asia, carries opposite, lanceolate to ovate leaves, tough-textured, and rich green in colour. After pollination, the white flowers develop into black berries. The reddish-brown trunk becomes slightly furrowed with age.

The myrtle is very hardy and suitable for beginners.

Position: a sunny or partially shaded spot near a window. From spring to autumn, the myrtle can also be kept out of doors. However, it must be allowed to accustom itself gradually to the sun. A myrtle that has spent the summer out of doors will also tolerate slight autumn frost. To be on the safe side, however, the plant should be brought back indoors in late autumn and placed in a cool, light position. However, many myrtles also flourish in a heated room if the temperature drops at night and the humidity level is not too low.

Soil: a mix of two parts fired clay particles, one part sand and one part potting compost. Other soil mixes are also suitable.

Watering: keep evenly moist. The plant should not become waterlogged under any circumstances. Ordinary tap water is quite suitable.

Feeding: as long as the plant is still developing, feed every two weeks from spring to summer with an organic fertilizer. A well-established myrtle bonsai should be fed once a month in order to encourage flowering. After the flowering season, the intervals between feeds can be extended.

Training: on young plants, new growth should be cut back once it has reached a length of about 10cm (4in) to encourage the branches to grow thicker. Depending on the branch's position in the crown, it should be trimmed back to between one and five leaf pairs.

Since new shoots usually grow upwards, wire has to be used to train a myrtle. One- and two-year-old branches are still flexible enough to bend. Older branches are very brittle and break easily, so great care is needed in training them. If larger branches are not wired but guyed down, there is a risk that they will be torn away from the trunk or break off altogether.

Acquiring a plant: myrtles are easily propagated from cuttings. Untrained plants, three to five years old, can be bought as pot plants in florists shops and garden centres. They can also often be bought as bonsais.

Pests: myrtles are susceptible to attack by scale insects.

Myrtus communis, about 12 years old, Bünger collection

Nandina domestica
Heavenly or sacred bamboo ○

This evergreen plant, a native of Japan and China, develops into a bush with multiple stems and pinnate foliage. The leaves are green in summer, red in autumn and winter. The small, white flowers, borne in large, loose panicles, develop later into red berries.

N. *domestica* is very difficult to train into a genuine tree shape since it is more like a bamboo in appearance.

Position: a well-lit spot all year round, with a few hours per day in the sun. In summer, the plant will be perfectly happy out of doors. As soon as the first autumn frosts are expected, it should be brought back inside and placed in an unheated room where the temperature is lower than 18°C (64°F).
Soil: the soil mix should not be too fine grained, so that any excess liquid from the frequent waterings the plant requires can drain away easily and the roots will not become waterlogged. A mix of two parts fired clay particles, one part coarse sand and one part potting compost is suitable. Two-thirds of the soil should be replaced every two years, with the roots being pruned at the same time.
Watering: N. *domestica* requires frequent watering in summer. In winter, the plant's needs depend to a large extent on room temperature and humidity level. Rainwater is to be preferred. If you have to use tap water, at least leave it to stand before using it.
Feeding: every two weeks from spring to autumn with an organic fertilizer. During the winter, monthly feeds will be sufficient.
Training: the plant's natural habit leaves little scope for major styling operations. New shoots always grow straight

Nandina domestica, *about five years old*

upwards. The plant is therefore best suited to the group or forest style.

Even after repeated pruning, the plant will not develop many side shoots. If new shoots grow taller than desired, they can be cut back right to the soil. After a while, the plant will put out new shoots that will also grow straight upwards. Young shoots can be easily trained with wire. Older wood is very hard and brittle.
Acquiring a plant: N. *domestica* can sometimes be bought in nurseries. Specialist bonsai shops do not always keep it in stock, but can usually supply it to order. It can also be propagated from cuttings.
Pests: N. *domestica* is susceptible to greenfly infestation.

Olea europaea
Olive   ○ – ◑

As it ages, this evergreen tree develops a gnarled, furrowed trunk. It is one of the oldest cultivated plants in the world, and is particularly widespread throughout Mediterranean regions. The leathery, lanceolate, opposite leaves, which vary considerably in length from variety to variety, are dark green on top and greyish-green on the underside.

The four-lobed, white flowers, borne in panicles, are followed by the fruits, which start off green and turn glossy black when fully ripe.

Provided an unheated room is available for the winter, olive trees can easily be kept as houseplants.

Position: an olive bonsai will flourish best in a sunny location, but can also be kept in partial shade. The tree's development can be greatly assisted by moving it out of doors in summer, either onto a balcony or into the garden. It should be brought inside again in autumn and placed in an unheated room where the temperature is between 5 and 18°C (41 and 64°F).

Soil: a mix of two parts fired clay particles and one part sand. Other soil mixes can also be used successfully.

Watering: as soon as the soil surface has dried out slightly, water with tap water that has been boiled or left to stand. If kept in conditions similar to those in its native habitat (cool, with a temperature of between 5 and 12°C (41 and 53°F)), it will require little water in winter. If it is kept in a heated room, it will need more.

Feeding: feed all year round with an organic or inorganic fertilizer. From the first new growth in spring to autumn, the tree needs to be fed every two weeks; in winter, monthly feeds are sufficient.

Training: the olive tree's natural habit will allow it to be trained into virtually any of the Japanese styles, with the broom and upright styles being the most popular.

Olive trees grow mainly in spring or autumn, i.e. during the periods of heaviest rainfall in its native habitat. With an established bonsai, new growth can be trimmed back to between one and three leaf pairs once the new shoot has reached a length of 5–10cm (2–4in). If larger limbs have to be removed at the beginning of the training process, this is best done in the spring, just as new shoots are emerging.

Two-year-old branches can be wired. However, if the bark is damaged, scars will remain visible for a long time.

Acquiring a plant: olive trees can be propagated from heel cuttings. Roughly trained specimens are sometimes available in bonsai shops. More rarely, olive trees can also be bought as young plants. Holidaymakers in Mediterranean-type regions will be able to buy the plant in local nurseries. Choose a smaller-leaved variety in preference to a larger-leaved one.

Pests: spider mite infestation can be fatal to olive trees, since it usually remains undetected. The first indication of spider mite attack is the development of deformed leaves, which later drop while still green. In cases of heavy infestation, very fine webs full of tiny creatures can be seen. Before attempting to treat any infestation, consult an expert, since most of the available insecticides have only a short-term effect.

Olea europaea, *about six years old, Caspary collection*

Pinus halepensis
Aleppo pine   ○

In its native habitat (the Mediterranean from Spain to the Near East), *P. halepensis* is cultivated for its nuts. It is able to tolerate very low levels of rainfall. The trunk, which in mature specimens is furrowed and reddish-brown, supports a sparse crown, the branches of which are characterized by frequent twists and turns. The long, soft needles, up to 15cm (6in) in length, are arranged in pairs on the branches. The female flowers develop into stalked, reddish-brown cones.

P. halepensis can be kept as an indoor bonsai only under certain conditions. It must spend some time every year in the open, and spend the winter in temperatures lower than 10°C (50°F). The humidity level must not fall below 50%.

Position: a bright, sunny spot is preferred. *P. halepensis* is easier to look after if it is shaded from the midday sun, since it would otherwise have to be watered frequently on hot days. Between May and September, it should be outside, in the garden or on a balcony. In winter, it is best kept in a cold conservatory, an unheated room indoors in which a window can be left open from time to time, or in a frost-free greenhouse in the garden.
Soil: a mix of two parts fired clay particles, one part sand and one part lava chippings. Two-thirds of the soil should be changed every two to three years, with the roots being pruned at the same time.
Watering: hard tap water is positively welcome. Young plants should be kept evenly moist, but not too wet. Older specimens tolerate brief periods of dryness, although young shoots will shrivel up.
Feeding: young plants should be fed every two weeks, older ones once a month with an organic or inorganic fertilizer. No feeding is required in winter.
Training: with the exception of the broom style, all styles can echo the tree's natural growth pattern. *P. halepensis* can be trained easily into the upright style. Older specimens develop relatively long needles, so the final height to be aimed for should be not less than 30cm (12in).

The branches remain flexible for a long time, and even three-year-old branches can still be shaped with wire. However, the wire must be checked at regular intervals: at certain times, the branches thicken very rapidly and there is a risk of the wire becoming too tight and damaging the bark. If this happens, it must be removed and, usually, replaced. The needles should be removed from wired sections of the tree, since they quickly turn brown and unsightly.

With young plants, new growth should be cut back once the shoots have reached a length of 15–20cm (6–8in). Shoots at the top of the tree should be pruned harder than those lower down.
Acquiring a plant: *P. halepensis is* sometimes sold as a bonsai in specialist shops. These are usually young trees, whose needles are still relatively short and quite distant. It can also be propagated from seeds.
Pests: *P. halepensis* is not very susceptible to pests.

Pinus halepensis, *about eight years old*

Pinus pinea
Umbrella or stone pine ○

The umbrella pine is one of the most common pines in Mediterranean regions. Its common name is derived from its characteristic dense, flat-topped head. The dark-brown trunk, tough and furrowed in older specimens, has reddish patches where the bark flakes off. The needles, which can be up to 20cm (8in) in length, are arranged in pairs on the branches, which start off green and then turn brown. The large fruits borne in the compact, roundish cones can be distinguished from those of other pines by their tiny, almost non-existent wings. *P. pinea* is one of the few conifers that can tolerate a centrally heated atmosphere, at least intermittently. However, attempts at styling will be unsuccessful unless the tree is placed outside during the growing season and can be kept sufficiently cold in winter to prevent any further growth.

Position: a bright, sunny location, shaded from the midday sun. In summer, the plant is best kept out of doors, either on a balcony or in the garden. In winter, it should be placed in an unheated room, where the humidity level should not fall below 50%. In winter, it will tolerate temperatures just above 0°C (32°F).
Soil: a mix of two parts fired clay particles, one part sand and one part lava chippings. Two-thirds of the soil should be replaced every two to three years, when the roots should be pruned.
Watering: in summer, the soil should be kept evenly moist, particularly with young plants. Temporary dryness is tolerated in winter. Ordinary tap water is quite satisfactory.

Feeding: every two to three weeks during the growing season with an organic or inorganic fertilizer. No feeding is necessary in winter.
Training: *P. pinea* is one of the few conifers whose natural growth pattern makes it best suited to the broom style, with its flat, broad crown. However, other styles are also perfectly feasible. The needles of the umbrella pine grow to a considerable length, and on young shoots it is not unusual to find very long needles next to shorter ones. In such case, the longer needles can be removed carefully by hand.

P. pinea should not be kept too small, so that the proportions remain acceptable. The trunk and branches of young trees remain flexible for a long time, and even three-year-old limbs can be shaped easily with wire. It is advisable to remove the needles from those parts of the tree that are to be trained in this way, so that they do not get caught up in the wire. The wire should not be too tight to prevent damage to the bark.

A tree wired during the winter can usually have its wire removed in mid-summer, although it may be necessary to replace it if the branches do not remain in the desired position. Sturdy branches on older specimens can also be guyed down for styling purposes.

Young shoots on plants that have not yet developed pairs of needles can be cut back once they have reached a length of 15–20cm (6–8in). New growth in the top of the crown should be pruned more severely than new shoots further down the tree. If older specimens are pruned back to wood already several years old, the remaining section of the branch should have some needles left on it, since otherwise there is no guarantee that new shoots will develop.

Pinus pinea, *young plant*

Acquiring a plant: umbrella pines can be propagated from their seeds, which are widely sold in food shops as pine nuts or kernels. Two-year-old specimens can often be bought just before Christmas.

Older specimens can be found in nurseries in Mediterranean-type regions. Ready-styled trees are very seldom seen. **Pests:** seedlings are very susceptible to fungal infestation if kept too damp.

Pistacia lentiscus
Mastic tree   ○ – ◑

This evergreen plant, which usually grows as a shrub, sometimes as a tree, is a native of the Mediterranean. It can frequently be found growing right on the coast. The leaves are alternate and pinnate, and the individual leaflets of this wild-growing plant can reach a length of 5cm (2in). The flowers emerge in dense clusters from the leaf axils. The female flowers give way to inedible fruits that are initially reddish and then black. Provided the atmospheric conditions in the room are suitable, the mastic tree can be considered an easy plant, suitable for a beginner to the art of bonsai.

Position: for preference, a light, partially shaded location. However, a mastic tree can also be placed by a sunlit window. Although it will tolerate a dry atmosphere, it will not thrive properly unless humidity is higher. In summer, it can be moved out of doors. It must be allowed to accustom itself to the sun gradually. In winter, an indoor location with a temperature lower than 18°C (64°F) is desirable, for example in the window of an unheated bedroom.

Soil: the soil can be a mix of loam and sand. Other well-draining soil mixes are also suitable, for example one consisting of two parts fired clay particles, one part sand and one part potting compost.

Watering: the mastic tree can be watered with hard tap water when the soil surface is still slightly moist.

Feeding: once a week between early spring and mid-autumn with an organic fertilizer. In winter, feed once a month.

Training: the pinnate foliage means a clearly defined structure is difficult to achieve, since the leaves usually grow uncontrollably in all directions. However, this problem can be solved if the tree is over 30cm (12in) by cutting back or completely removing individual leaves that obscure the design.

The mastic tree is usually trained into the broom or informal upright styles. However, other styles, such as the cascade or multiple-trunk styles, are also feasible.

One- to two-year-old branches can be wired easily. The wire must be checked regularly during the growing season. Since the plant grows most quickly in spring and autumn, these are also the periods of most frequent pruning. New growth should be allowed to reach a length of 20cm (8in) before being cut back to between one and five leaves, depending on the shoot's position in the crown. The new shoot that will emerge in about three weeks will grow in the direction determined by the leaf closest to the cut. Older, well-developed plants can be pruned earlier, to prevent younger limbs from growing too thick and to promote twiggy growth in the outer crown area.

Acquiring a plant: the mastic tree can be propagated from cuttings. It is commercially available only as a so-called bonsai. However, such specimens are usually very young, untrained plants that have merely been placed in a bonsai container.

Pests: P. lenticus falls prey to scale insects and mealy bugs. In obstinate cases, help should be sought from a bonsai specialist.

Pistacia lentiscus, *about eight years old*

Podocarpus macrophyllus
Chinese podocarpus ○

This evergreen, dioecious (male and female flowers on separate plants) conifer, a native of southern Japan and southern China, bears large, broad needles arranged in dense spirals on its brown stems, which by their second year have become tough and slightly furrowed. The seed is surrounded by a fleshy, purplish receptacle. In Asia, it adorns many gardens and temple precincts.

   P. macrophyllus is the only conifer that is frequently cultivated as a bonsai.

Position: by a light, sunny window. From spring to autumn, *P. macrophyllus* can be placed out of doors, although it must be allowed to accustom itself gradually to direct sunlight. If the plant is kept outside until the autumn, it should spend the winter in an unheated

Podocarpus macrophylus

room at temperatures between 10 and 18°C (50 and 64°F). *P. macrophyllus* bonsais kept indoors all year round will also tolerate a heated room in winter.
Soil: a well-draining mix of three parts fired clay particles, one part sand and one part potting compost. Two-thirds of the soil should be changed every two to three years.
Watering: keep evenly moist. Ordinary tap water is quite suitable.
Feeding: every three weeks from spring to early autumn with an organic or inorganic fertilizer. Do not feed in winter, in order to prevent new growth.
Training: all styles are feasible, except the broom style. *P. macrophyllus* is usually trained into the upright or cascade styles.

   Imported specimens are often shaped with steel wire, which very quickly becomes ingrown. This wire should be removed as soon as possible, because it leaves slight rust marks on the trunk. As a rule, however, the branches will not have been shaped as desired and will have to be wired again with aluminium wire. Powerful limbs can be persuaded into shape through the use of suspended wiring.

   Once new shoots have reached a length of 10cm (4in), cut them back to 1–5cm (0.4–2in). If you wish to encourage twiggy growth, remove older needles so that new buds will form.
Acquiring a plant: *P. macrophyllus* can be propagated from cuttings. However, because of its slow rate of growth, it would be better to start with an older specimen. Such plants can sometimes be bought in bonsai shops, and untrained young plants are sometimes sold in florists shops.
Pests: there are no known pests with a particular predilection for *P. macrophyllus.*

Portulacaria afra
Purslane tree　　　　○ – ◑

This succulent, a native of South Africa, grows as a shrub or small tree. Its fleshy limbs carry opposite, thick, bright green leaves that contain water storage tissues. The stem or trunk is initially smooth but after a few years develops a dark brown, furrowed bark.

P. afra is undemanding and is one of the plants that can be recommended for beginners.

Position: a light, sunny spot all year round. From spring (beware of late frosts!) to autumn, the plant can occupy a partially shaded to sunny spot out of doors. It should be brought indoors for the winter, either to an unheated room or even to a heated room, provided the heating goes off at night.

Soil: a well-draining mix, low in humus, of three parts fired clay particles, one part lava chippings, and one part fine gravel.

Watering: P. afra needs regular watering in summer, although it will also tolerate short periods of dryness. If kept in a cool room in winter, it should not be watered until the soil surface has dried out. Ordinary tap water can be used.

Feeding: every two weeks in summer with a fertilizer low in nitrogen (e.g. cactus fertilizer). If it is kept in a cool room in winter, it will not need feeding. If it is in a room that is heated during the day, then it should be fed once a month.

Training: if training begins early, all styles are feasible. The broom and upright styles are popular choices. Branches no thicker than a finger can be wired. However, the wire must be frequently removed and renewed, since the branches thicken quickly. New growth should be cut back to one to two leaf pairs once the shoot has reached a length of 5cm (2in). New shoots should be allowed to grow longer only in those places where new branches are to grow. This also applies to the leader, if the tree is supposed to grow taller. The cuts do not usually need any special treatment, since they soon dry up and also because the edges of the wound will roll over and heal flush with the trunk.

Acquiring a plant: P. afra can be easily propagated from cuttings. Young plants can be bought in florists shops. It can also be bought as a bonsai in various stages of development.

Pests: root lice are not unknown in P. afra. They must be treated, since they will migrate to other plants. Specialist advice should be sought.

Portulacaria afra, *about eight years old*

Punica granatum
Pomegranate   ○ – ◑

This deciduous plant, a native of the Mediterranean, has oblong to lanceolate leaves that in their native habitat become very robust, almost tough. It grows as a shrub or tree, often with thorny branches, and produces large, red, cup-shaped flowers, from which the familiar, very tasty fruits develop. The small-leaved variety *P. granatum* 'Nana' grows as a shrub and produces large numbers of smaller flowers of the same shape. The fruits are correspondingly smaller and are not suitable for eating. Some cultivars bear flowers of a different shape and colour. The pomegranate can be recommended to fans of flowering bonsais who have a cool room where the plant can be placed in winter.

Position: in summer, it is best kept in a sunny to partially shaded location out of doors. However, it can also be kept successfully inside, in as light a spot as possible. Since the flowers emerge at the ends of branches and the tree has a more compact habit when kept outside, a pomegranate placed out of doors is more likely to bear flowers not too far outside the crown area than one kept indoors. In winter, a pomegranate is best kept in a frost-free but cold location. It can also be put in an unheated room.
Soil: a mix of two parts fired clay particles, one part sand and one part potting compost. Other soil mixes can also be used successfully. Young plants should be repotted every one to two years. Older trees can be repotted less often.
Watering: in the warmer months, the plant can be kept fairly moist. In winter,

when it has shed its leaves, it needs only moderate watering. If it has to be kept in a warm room for want of anywhere more suitable, however, it will need more water. Ordinary tap water is quite suitable.
Feeding: feed generously with an organic fertilizer. Inorganic fertilizers should be used with care. Do not feed in winter at all.
Training: the tree's natural habit makes all styles feasible. One- and two-year old branches can be styled easily by wiring. Older branches will have to be guyed down.

The plant should be pruned hard before any new shoots emerge in spring, to make way for the new growth.

Young plants that are still developing should be trimmed back to between two and five leaf pairs, depending on the branch's position in the crown, once new shoots have reached a length of 15cm (6in). More mature trees can be pruned at an earlier stage.

In general, care should be taken to ensure that most of the flower buds are also removed when the first new growth is cut back in the spring. So if you attach a lot of importance to the flowers, you will have to compromise a little on the shape of your bonsai and delay the first pruning until after the flowers have appeared, which usually happens in mid-summer.
Acquiring a plant: the plant can be propagated by sowing seeds from the fruits. To do this, place some pips in water for a few days until they begin to ferment. Remove the flesh and sow immediately. Pomegranates can also be propagated easily from cuttings.

Its profuse and attractive flowers make *P. granatum* 'Nana' a very popular plant, and it is often sold in bloom. The actual fruit tree, *P. granatum*, can also be

Punica granatum, *about eight years old, Thönnessen collection*

bought as a bonsai, but will flower only if it gets enough sun, and even then only sparsely. The various cultivars can be bought in Mediterranean-type regions. **Pests:** pomegranates kept indoors are often attacked by whitefly. This pest is very difficult to control and should be left to an expert. Outdoors, pomegranates are also susceptible to greenfly infestation.

Quercus ilex
Evergreen or holm oak ○

This evergreen tree is a native of the Mediterranean region, and its smooth, greyish trunk, which becomes attractively corrugated with age, supports a rounded head. The alternate, leathery leaves are usually toothed.

Although the evergreen oak is a very attractive tree, it is seldom cultivated as a bonsai.

Quercus ilex, *about ten years old*

Position: in summer, the evergreen oak should be kept in a bright, sunny spot, preferably out of doors. If it is taken outside in spring, it must be allowed to accustom itself gradually to the sun. Once it has become acclimatized, however, it can spend the whole day in direct sunlight. In winter, it is best kept indoors, in a light, unheated room near a window.

Soil: a mix of two parts fired clay particles, one part sand and one part potting compost. Other soil mixes can also be used, provided they are loose and open enough in texture. Young plants should be repotted every one to two years, older plants less frequently.

Quercus suber, *about eight years old, still without bark*

Watering: ordinary tap water can be used. The evergreen oak should be kept evenly moist, but is tolerant of considerable variation in its watering schedule. It is better to water sparingly than to excess.

Feeding: every two weeks during the growing season with an organic or inorganic fertilizer. Do not feed at all in winter.

Training: the tree's natural habit means all styles are feasible. One- to two-year old branches can be trained easily by wiring. Older branches should be guyed down to avoid bark damage. In young plants, new shoots should be allowed to grow to a length of 20cm (8in) before being cut back, in order to encourage the branches to grow thicker. Cut back to between two and five leaves, depending on the branch's position in the crown. Older trees can be pruned at an earlier stage.

Acquiring a plant: evergreen oaks are only occasionally sold as young plants. Older plants and ready-styled bonsais are almost impossible to find. The best way of collecting starting material is on

holiday, in the form of seedlings. Older plants are very difficult to transport.
Pests: the evergreen oak is not susceptible to pests.

Quercus suber
Cork oak ○

This is probably the best-known oak from the Mediterranean region, and is cultivated largely for its thick, rugged, corky bark, which provides the cork of commerce. This evergreen tree has alternate leaves that closely resemble those of the evergreen oak, although they are much less prominently toothed. The rugged bark and relatively small leaves make it well suited to styling as a bonsai. Unfortunately, it is not easy to reproduce the conditions in which it thrives best: plenty of sun out of doors in summer, and a frost-free, cool winter.

Position: bright all year round, with several hours of sunlight. From late spring to autumn, the cork oak can remain out of doors, on a balcony or in the garden. As soon as the first frosts are expected, it should be brought indoors and placed in a bright, cool spot.
Soil: a well draining mix of two parts fired clay particles, one part sand or fine gravel and one part potting compost. With young plants, two-thirds of the soil should be replaced every one to two years. Older bonsais can be left longer in the same soil.
Watering: in the warmer months, the cork oak should be kept fairly moist with tap water, otherwise it will fail to grow. In winter, do not water until the soil surface has dried out slightly.
Feeding: from early spring to mid-autumn, young plants should be fed generously, at least every two weeks, with organic or inorganic fertilizer. This

will encourage growth, and with it the development of the bark. Older plants, in which the bark is already well developed, can be fed less frequently. Do not feed at all in winter.
Training: the broom and upright styles are closest to the tree's natural habit, and it can be easily trimmed and wired into these styles. If you have a more radical style in mind, training will have to begin early.

One- and two-year-old branches can be wired without difficulty. However, wire placed in the spring will often have to be removed after three months because it has become too tight. If the branch has not yet grown into the required position, it will have to be rewired. Older limbs should be guyed down. New shoots on young plants still being trained should be allowed to reach a length of 20cm (8in) before being cut back to between one and five leaves, depending on the branch's position in the crown. Older, well-established plants can be pruned earlier.
Acquiring a plant: very occasionally, you may see a cork oak for sale as a pot plant. Seeds gathered in the wild are best sown immediately, with the seedlings being kept during the winter in an unheated room. Propagation from cuttings is not easy, but possible nevertheless. Ready-styled specimens are a rarity.
Pests: the cork oak is not very susceptible to pests.

Rosmarinus officinalis
Common rosemary ○

This aromatic, evergreen shrub from the Mediterranean has narrow, needle-shaped leaves, bluish-green above and white and hairy beneath. The bright blue flowers emerge all year round from the leaf axils. The trunk and older branches have grey, conspicuously rough bark. It is this bark that makes *R. officinalis* a very interesting plant for bonsai enthusiasts. However, a little experience is called for.

Position: light and sunny. In summer, it is best kept out of doors. In winter, it can be placed in an unheated room where the humidity is not too low.
Soil: a mix of equal parts of fired clay particles, sand and potting compost. Half the soil should be changed every two years, with the roots being pruned at the same time.
Watering: water moderately, but keep evenly moist. If the soil is too damp, large parts of the root mass will die off. Tap water can be used.
Feeding: every three weeks from mid-spring to mid-autumn. Do not feed in winter unless the temperature gets above 16°C (61°F). An organic or inorganic fertilizer can be used.
Training: *R. officinalis* is also suitable for cultivation as a miniature bonsai. All styles are feasible. The easiest one to achieve successfully is the broom style, which merely requires careful pruning but no wiring.

If you have other styles in mind, training should begin early. One-year-old branches can be wired; older ones should be guyed down to avoid damage to the bark.

With mature bonsais, new shoots can be cut back to between 1 and 3cm (0.4 and 1in) from a length of 5–10cm (2–4in), depending on the branch's position in the crown. Young plants that are still developing should not be pruned until the shoots have reached a length of 15cm (6in). Weaker branches can also be simply left to grow so that they grow stronger.
Acquiring a plant: *R. officinalis* can be propagated from cuttings. Young plants for use as herbs can be bought as pot plants. You should not dig up plants you come across on holiday. They seldom get used to their new environment and die off very quickly, weakened by the loss of roots. Older specimens can sometimes be bought in nurseries in Mediterranean-type areas; they will adapt more easily to new conditions. Ready-styled trees can occasionally be bought in specialist shops.
Pests: *R. officinalis* is not very susceptible to attack by pests.

Sageretia thea
Sageretia ○ – ◑

This evergreen shrub (syn. *S. theezans*), a native of Asia, has alternate, oval, green leaves, borne on russet branches. The smooth, dark to light brown bark peels off at regular intervals in large patches, giving the trunk a beautiful patchy effect. The plant produces white flowers in small clusters.

Sageretias are one of the most frequently imported indoor bonsais. Since they usually arrive in very loamy soil, beginners may find them problematic.

Position: light to partially shaded. In summer, sageretias can be placed

Rosmarinus officinalis, *young plant*

Sageretia thea, *about forty years old, Rüger collection*

and one part peat is recommended for a good balance.

Watering: use tap water that has been left to stand. Water when the soil surface is still just moist.

Feeding: feed with an organic or inorganic fertilizer once every week or every two weeks during the growing season. Feed once a month in winter.

Training: all styles are feasible. If you use a young plant or even a cutting as your starting material, the plant can be trimmed into the desired shape. Only young, thin branches can be shaped with wire. Older branches break very easily. Cut back new shoots once they have reached a length of 10–15cm (4–6in). If a new shoot is to develop into a new branch, it can be left to grow to a length of 30–40cm (12–16in). In this way, it will grow thicker more quickly. Depending on the branch's position in the crown, such shoots should be cut back to between one and five leaves.

Acquiring a plant: plants bought in shops have usually not been styled. Sageretias can be propagated easily from cuttings, which soon grow quickly into handsome little trees if cared for properly. Seeds are very difficult to acquire, since it is very difficult to persuade sageterias to flower and therefore to fruit.

Pests: if the loamy soil becomes waterlogged and compressed, fungal infestations are possible. Brown spots on leaves and leaf margins are an indication of this. Poor ventilation encourages mildew. Sageterias are also attacked frequently by whitefly.

outside. In winter, they are best kept in an unheated room where the temperature is between 15 and 18°C (59 and 64°F).

Soil: a mix of equal parts of fired clay particles, peat and sand. If you buy a bonsai growing in loamy soil, it should be repotted as soon as possible. Sageretias do not react so sensitively to root pruning as the Fukien tea, for example. Repotting is not, therefore, as problematic. Nevertheless, the new soil should still be fairly loamy; a mix of two parts fired clay particles, one part sand,

Schefflera actinophylla ○ – ◑
Queensland umbrella or octopus tree

This tree, a native of Australia and New Guinea, bears alternate, digitate leaves. Schefflera is very familiar as a houseplant notable for its durability. Its large leaves and general disinclination to produce new branches, however, make it not such a good choice for bonsai enthusiasts. It is very difficult to train it to grow like a European or Japanese tree.

Position: light and warm but shaded from the sun. Schefflera can be put outside in the warmer months, but should not be placed in direct sunlight. In winter, the humidity level should not fall below 40%, otherwise the plant will become more susceptible to attack by pests.
Soil: a mix of equal parts of fired clay particles, sand and potting compost. Schefflera bonsai can also be grown in ordinary garden soil.

Schefflera actinophylla, *about five years old*

Watering: tap water is perfectly suitable. Water as soon as the soil surface is dry.
Feeding: feed with organic or inorganic fertilizer every two weeks from spring to autumn, once a month in winter.
Training: even when trained as a bonsai, Schefflera will not adopt a recognisably tree-like shape. Its numerous aerial roots and lack of secondary branches make it look very like a mangrove. It is very difficult to train it in any of the established styles. The branches can be shaped with wire even when relatively old. If you are aiming for one of the classic bonsai styles, you will have no choice but to resort to wire. However, thick branches should be guyed down to protect the bark.

Pruning should begin once the new growth has reached a length of 10–20cm (4–8in). It is frequently the case that only one new shoot develops at the tip of the stem after pruning. To encourage new branches to grow, this shoot should be repeatedly removed until the plant puts out some lateral shoots. Leaf pruning sometimes encourages the development of lateral shoots as well.
Acquiring a plant: Schefflera can be easily propagated from cuttings, although it is quicker to buy a pot plant for cultivation as a bonsai. Ready-styled plants can occasionally be bought in bonsai shops.
Pests: Schefflera is a favourite target for scale insects.

Serissa foetida
Tree of a thousand stars ○ – ◑

This evergreen shrub, a native of South-East Asia, has small, ovate, opposite leaves. The small, white flowers, single in the typical form, emerge individually from the numerous leaf axils. Even in young plants, the grey bark peels off in strips.

The plant is very often sold as a young bonsai, and is very popular for its magnificent blooms. However, it is unsuitable for beginners, and even experienced bonsai enthusiasts are seldom able to keep it for any great length of time. Older specimens, at least 40cm (16in) in height, whose stems have already reached a certain thickness, are an exception to this rule.

Position: a light spot all year round, but one that is shaded from direct sun. In summer, the plant can be moved out of doors. In winter, it is best kept in an unheated room.

Soil: almost any well-drained soil mix is suitable. With the correct feeding, it is possible to use just fired clay particles. Once you have chosen a mix, however, you should stick to it. Two-thirds of the soil should be changed every one to two years.

Watering: use rainwater or tap water that has been left to stand. *S. foetida* should be kept as evenly moist as possible. Check the soil surface at regular intervals, and water the plant as soon as it is only slightly moist. It needs less water when it has lost a few leaves, after a move or in autumn. It is susceptible to fungal infestation if it gets too wet. There is no treatment that will get rid of the fungi!

Feeding: every two weeks from late spring to late autumn, once a month in winter. Use organic or inorganic fertilizer.

Training: all styles are feasible. The so-called exposed root style, in which the roots support the tree as if it were on stilts, seems to be a very popular choice.

Shoots should be trimmed once they have reached a length of 10cm (4in). Depending on the branch's position in the crown, cut back to between one and five leaf pairs. Limbs up to three years old can be styled with wire. Older branches should be guyed down carefully.

Acquiring a plant: specimens of various ages and stages of development are widely available in shops and garden centres. It can also be easily propagated from cuttings, which quickly develop into small trees.

Pests: any of the pests that commonly attack houseplants may attack *S. foetida*. However, none of them has a particular predilection for the plant. In most cases, unsuitable environmental conditions are responsible for the plant's death.

Serissa foetida, *about ten years old*

Ulmus parvifolia
Chinese elm   ○

The name 'Chinese elm' is used to denote several evergreen elms from various parts of Asia that have small, alternate, leathery leaves, dark green in colour and oval in shape. The dark-grey trunk has smooth bark that furrows slightly with age.

Although the tree is quite often attacked by spider mites, it is one of the hardiest trees used by bonsai growers and can be successfully cultivated by beginners who have a cool room available for the winter.

Position: a bright and sunny spot all year round. From spring to autumn, the Chinese elm will be quite happy out of doors, although it must be allowed to accustom itself gradually to direct sunlight. Once outdoors, it will withstand strong wind and heavy downpours. The most suitable location in winter is an unheated room.
Soil: a mix of two parts fired clay particles, one part sand and one part potting compost. Other soil mixes can also be used successfully.
Watering: water the plant as soon as the soil surface has dried out. The Chinese elm will tolerate hard tap water.
Feeding: feed with an organic or inorganic fertilizer once every two weeks from early spring to mid-autumn. In winter, if the plant is kept in a cool location, feed once a month.
Training: all styles are feasible. One- and two-year-old branches can be wired easily. Since wire can leave visible traces on more powerful branches, they should be persuaded to grow in the desired position by the use of suspended wiring.

In young plants, new shoots should be cut back once they have reached a length of 10cm (4in). In older, well developed specimens, pruning can be done at an earlier stage. Depending on their position in the crown, new shoots should be cut back to between one and five leaves.
Acquiring a plant: Chinese elms can be propagated easily from cuttings and soon develop into imposing trees. Specimens of all ages and stages of development can be purchased in shops and garden centres.
Pests: the Chinese elm frequently falls prey to spider mites, particularly in winter if the room in which it is placed is too warm and the humidity level too low.

Ulmus parvifolia, *about twenty years old, Meyer-Horn collection*

Index

Where there is more than one page reference, the number(s) in **bold** refer to a more detailed passage. Page numbers in *italics* refer to illustrations.